Living Like a Child

Living Like a Child

· ·

Learn, Live, and Teach
CREATIVELY

ENRIQUE C. FELDMAN

Redleaf Press®
www.redleafpress.org
800-423-8309

Published by Redleaf Press
10 Yorkton Court
St. Paul, MN 55117
www.redleafpress.org

First edition 2011
Cover design by Jim Handrigan
Cover photograph © Fuse/PunchStock
Interior typeset in Sabon and designed by Douglas Schmitz
Printed in the United States of America
18 17 16 15 14 13 12 11   1 2 3 4 5 6 7 8

Library of Congress Cataloging-in-Publication Data
Feldman, Enrique C.
    Living like a child : learn, live, and teach creatively / Enrique C. Feldman.
— 1st ed.
        p. cm.
    Includes bibliographical references.
    ISBN 978-1-60554-033-7 (alk. paper)
    1. Creative teaching.   I. Title.
LB1062.6.F45 2011
371.1—dc22
                                    2011008019

Printed on acid-free paper

For Nicky, Samantha, and Charles

Contents

Acknowledgments

❦ ❦ ❦ ❦ ❦ ❦ ❦

I TAKE GREAT PLEASURE in thanking Dr. David Woods, dean of the School of Fine Arts at the University of Connecticut, for his inspiration when I was a student at the University of Arizona. David taught me to play and learn with young children, and he encouraged me to redefine *lesson plan* to include improvisation and flexibility as integral parts. I also thank my friends and colleagues Debbie Clement, Rachelle Cohen, Candace Mazur, and Rick Wamer. Collaborating with them has truly been an honor. I thank the Bergen family and Assessment Technology Inc. for reintroducing me to the early childhood world and entrusting me with the education of so many teachers. I deeply thank Fritz Kaenzig and Dan Perantoni for teaching me so much as a young artist, most notably, how to strive for excellence. In addition, I am grateful to the late Robert Fountain, my colleague at the University of Wisconsin–Madison. He taught me that energy exists at all ages and that facial expressions can transform a performance. I cherish having sung Bach's *St. Matthew Passion* and Bernstein's *Chichester Psalms* under his direction; the experience changed me as a musician. I am also thankful to my high school band director Dr. Steve Steele of Normal, Illinois, who taught me that everything is relative, and my high school English teacher Tommy Harper, who profoundly shaped my life and introduced me to having a passion for words. A special thanks to Jean Cook for her artistic editing and courage to make bold suggestions and to David Heath for his support and his passion for quality.

I give a very special thanks to the legendary Mimi Brodsky Chenfeld, who has been guiding young children for more than half a century and continues to do so. Her courage to "simply and lovingly play" with children and adults in ways that create lifelong learners has been an inspiration to many. Thank you, Mimi, for reminding me how to be myself with children, for helping me teach with reckless joy, and for touching the lives of all of us in Arizona. I give a very special thanks to Dr. Carroll Rinehart, another living legend in the arts-education world. Thank you, Carroll, for your Yoda-like perspectives on education, life, and love and for illuminating the circle of growth, trust, risk, and affirmation. Thank you for spending so many hours with me and making me think more deeply. Without ever meaning to, you reminded me of my calling and inspired me with the twinkle in your eye and the story you are now able to tell without breaking down.

Finally, I give my most intimate thanks to my family. I am grateful to my parents for always loving me and for opening the door to the world of music and education. I thank my father for teaching me perseverance and my mother for her kindness and encouragement. I thank my brother Ted for his loyalty, friendship, and the many games of chess and glasses of wine we have shared. I thank Charles for always loving me, my children, and my wife. I thank my son, Nicky (eleven), my daughter, Samantha (fifteen), and my lifelong love and (amazingly young) wife, Marie. They have shaped me and have allowed me to shape them. My intensely artistic daughter has taught me a lot, including how to listen and how to let things come to me when they are ready. My utterly joyful and talented son continues to remind me of what unconditional love is and how a big heart is the answer to most of life's questions. And to Marie, there are simply no words to suffice. A glance, a breath, a scent, and I am suspended in light. You are my greatest champion and, without exception, you have been there for me with the one thing that fuels me indefinitely—loving me.

Introduction

AT AN EARLY AGE, I thought I knew what I wanted to do. I wanted to be a band director and thought I would be one for all of my life. What I "knew" as a young man, however, was only a glimpse of the path ahead. Focused, I flew through school and won a teaching position at a major university at a young age. In my position as a university band director, I went to high schools to promote music education and to recruit students. I sometimes chose to visit nearby middle schools and elementary schools. Eventually, I chose to visit preschools as well. I really didn't have to visit the young children—they were too young to recruit for my college program—but I enjoyed these experiences so much that, over time, I felt the need to be with them more often.

As we mature, and in response to our growing experiences, many of us begin to ask questions about ourselves and our lives. Fortunately, I was open to exploring these questions and open to change, which has led to opportunities. In my work with young children, I rediscovered my youthful, happy self. They gave back to me as much as I gave to them, and they continue to do so. When children hug you, there are no strings attached. When children look at you and say kind words, they mean what they say. When children tell you something sad, there is no mistaking that they want to be comforted. There are no politics when speaking to young children. Young children embrace playing, learning, and loving.

The Nature of Children

Children are, by their very nature, outstanding teachers. Consider the young children in your life, the impact you have on them, and the impact they have on you. Additionally, think about the adults in your life and what improvements might occur if they decided to live more like children: Children embrace each minute of play as if it were an Olympic moment. Children understand truth, honesty, and beauty. Children love unconditionally and understand the qualities that define us human beings—compassion, truth, and justice. Children sometimes ask amazingly deep questions that stop us in our tracks and force us to think. Stop just long enough in your day to observe a young child, and you'll likely smile or laugh. You might even do both. As adults, we must relearn how to live like children.

Children understand that people are defined by how they treat others. Just because we treat people well, however, does not mean we will be treated the same way in return. Out of this fear, many adults stop really interacting; they just go through the motions without investing in people or moments. People who lose the ability to truly connect end up living without passion or creativity. We can help children hold on to their instinctive ability to connect by giving them environments that encourage creativity and connection through the arts. These kinds of environments lead to improved academic and social-emotional growth. In this book, you will find arts-based, holistic facilitating techniques that will help you foster this growth.

My Life as a Child

As a young boy, my maternal grandmother, Nana Cañez, often told me, "Everything you touch turns to gold." She loved me, and I knew she loved me, but if strangers witnessed her saying those words, they'd think I was in trouble. Nana Cañez was a gruff, no-nonsense, pick-yourself-up-off-the-ground-and-stop-your-crying sort of nana. When

Master Teaching Principles

IN ANY PROFESSION, SOME INDIVIDUALS are of average competence, others are above average, and others are below average. Some individuals in every field become great, or true masters of their profession. I refer to teachers at this high level as *master teachers*. I believe the early childhood profession can become a field where a majority of teachers become master teachers.

Master teachers do more than share knowledge and promote academic achievement. They guide children to learn how to learn and help children develop internal motivation to achieve. Master teachers bring concepts such as compassion, truth, and service into education and often have an innate ability to connect emotionally with students, earning their trust in the process. These teachers do not live vicariously through children—forcing children to pursue the teacher's goals and interests. Instead, master teachers use children's natural interests to engage open-ended discussions in width (content based) and depth (connecting content to concepts), encouraging children to think aloud to start the process of critical thinking. Master teachers take risks by sharing control of a discussion's direction with children, allowing diverse thoughts to sometimes collide, and improvising as a topic area evolves or breaks down. Master teachers trust children's energy and creativity because they know that when a student is fully engaged in creating, the peripheral noise of life goes away and inner joy and meaning remain.

Teachers who rise to this high level of mastery possess many specialized skills. In chapters 1 through 5 of this book, I present the five underlying principles and critical elements to developing these skills, based on my experiences with young children and master early childhood educators. I refer to these five underlying elements as the Master Teaching Principles:

1. Honor your master teachers.

2. Teach to all learning styles.

3. Ask questions to encourage critical-thinking skills.

4. Improvise to foster creativity.

5. Teach topics in width and depth.

These Master Teaching Principles are each important on their own, but they also build on one another. Together they will help you powerfully and gently guide young children to realize their full potential. At the same time, and in conjunction with the Life Learning Techniques in part 2, these principles will help you live and teach with the energy and unclouded vision of a child—with creativity, inquisitiveness, and a desire to explore. Master teachers are childlike in many positive ways, and our children, if we pay attention, are often master teachers.

Taking Risks to Encourage Critical Thinking

For master teachers and all creative thinkers, risk is part of the daily ritual of learning and teaching, the gains of which are measured over a long period. As adults, we must remind ourselves not to get stuck in routine and not to stop exploring. Choosing to simply "graze where we know there is grass" is void of risk, and the potential gain is small.

We should not spend our energy asking children questions that only satisfy ourselves and our comfort zones: questions that only feed our egos, follow a strict lesson plan, or have readily available answers. Some of the best questions have no simple answers. Some have no quantifiable answers at all. We should be careful not to answer questions for children just because we think we know the answers. Instead, we should ask more questions based on children's cues and take a risk by going wherever they lead. This kind of reflective dialogue between guide and student leads directly to critical thinking. At the same time, the dialogue affirms students because they become a significant voice in the discussion and its direction. Affirming children means relinquishing some control.

Master teachers get to know each child so they can improvise and encourage in ways that will best communicate to that child, even when it means taking a risk and teaching in a new way. Sometimes knowing children means honoring the three basic learning styles—visual, auditory, and kinesthetic—so we can invite each child to love learning and strive for excellence. Honoring all learning styles makes each learner feel wanted, cared for, and part of the team in the classroom and at home. It gives them confidence to take risks of their own by thinking critically and creatively. Simultaneously, honoring the learning styles helps you expand your skills as a guide and forces you to improvise to help children enter the critical-thinking zone.

Master teachers take risks by grabbing opportunities to teach in depth as well as in width, even if the direction of discussion falls outside the lesson plan. Much of what we see in traditional classroom settings is teaching and learning in width; that is, with a great deal of breadth. Teaching and learning in depth means taking a portion of the content and seeing it from different perspectives, making the content come to life. More to the point, teaching in width and depth is all about connecting content to concepts, which is impossible without critical thinking on the part of the teacher and children.

When you take risks to encourage critical thinking, you end up having meaningful conversations with children by default. When you are in a classroom of three-, four-, and five-year-olds, for example, you could choose to read a book, guide all of the responses, and shut down any unwanted responses—but this is not masterful teaching. You could, instead, choose to read a book multiple times and add something different each time you read. As the children become familiar with the book—and assuming they love the story—a masterful teacher begins to ask questions. The questions might be simple at first, such as "What happens next?" Eventually, the master teacher might begin to ask questions related to actions, consequences, and emotions, such as "Why is the mama bear sad?" These kinds of questions push children to think in new ways and push teachers to listen and improvise, fostering critical-thinking skills for everyone involved.

Challenging Ourselves

Children have a lot of natural energy. By using our ears, our eyes, and our ability to improvise within a lesson plan, we can help children use the energy they have while simultaneously helping them improve their self-regulation skills to remain calm and focused. To be the best guides for children, we must also take care of ourselves and stay in good enough health to keep up with young children's energy. Being tired cannot be an excuse for failing to invite kinesthetic learners to engage in activities. We must rise to the challenge of being like children, sharing their energy, and creating educational environments that are so enticing that learning becomes a natural part of each child's life and our own.

Connecting with a child as a master teacher, whether in your classroom or at home, is one of the best feelings on earth. When you do this, you are shaping the future. One of my favorite words in Spanish is *desafío*. It is a beautiful word, and it rolls off the tongue. The paradox is that this beautiful word means *challenge*. Challenge yourself to be more than just good or great. Challenge yourself to be masterful.

Chapter 1

Honor Your
Master Teachers

M aster teachers are both examples and guides. Think about the master teachers who have affected you so deeply that you will remember them throughout your life. For example, I remember and thank the following people:

- Mr. James Andrews of San Diego, California, my piano teacher from age four to twelve. He taught me the importance of patience, understanding, and encouragement. On more than one occasion, he watched *Sesame Street* with me before my lesson because, at age four, I was sometimes "not in the mood" for my lesson.

- Colonel Edward Zaharia of Tucson, Arizona, my high school government teacher. He challenged how I thought and had high expectations of me.

- Mr. Dan Perantoni, of Bloomington, Indiana, my tuba teacher from late high school through my undergraduate years. He taught me the importance of friendship and the need for teachers to be able to say the same thing a hundred different ways.

- Mr. Fritz Kaenzig, of Ann Arbor, Michigan, my tuba teacher during graduate school. He pushed me harder than any other teacher, taught me to look within myself for the drive to succeed, and loved me in the process.

I honor the master teachers in my life by remembering them, and by remembering them, I continue to learn from them. Even now, years after I formally studied with any of them, I still have moments when I truly grasp, for the first time, something they taught me. They still serve as guides for me. When I reflect about these teachers, I realize that *how* they taught was more important than *what* they taught; they improvised, challenged me with linear and abstract questions, encouraged my creative nature, and taught me in width and depth. They used these principles to help me develop my self-concept so I would be able to create my own path later in life. I have been fortunate to have had many exemplary mentors in my life, and I can look to these teachers as examples of the teacher I want to be.

What teachers or mentors have been important in your life? Using the Key Teachers List that follows, make a list of the key people in your development and overall success. These master teachers can be from any part of your life, childhood or adulthood, and from any sphere, personal or professional. They can be any age. Many times children affect us deeply, teaching us with their innocent and courageous outlook on life. Under each name on your list, write what you have learned from that person. Then write at least one thing you do better today because of that individual.

Key Teachers List

Teacher

_____

What I learned from this person

_____

_____

_____

One thing I do well today because of this person

_____

_____

_____

Teacher

_____

What I learned from this person

_____

_____

_____

One thing I do well today because of this person

_____

_____

_____

Review your list of mentors and teachers and what you have learned from them. Think about how you might use these teachers as examples for your own work with children. Then consider this related and important question: who are you mentoring? Write down the names of the people you mentor on the Impact List that follows. Even if you don't yet consider yourself a master teacher—becoming a master teacher is a process, and many master teachers never think of themselves as such—you still impact the people around you. Once you have completed the list, ask yourself the "big question": what kind of people do you want these individuals to be?

Impact List

Who am I mentoring?

_____

_____

_____

_____

_____

What kind of people do I want these individuals to be?

_____

_____

_____

_____

_____

We can choose what kind of teachers we want to be, mediocre or masterful. If your answer to the second question on the Impact List is what I expect, then take responsibility for being the best example and guide you can be for our next generation.

Defining Masterful Teaching

Those who teach masterfully understand that loving and learning are two-way streets. Master teachers balance child-initiated and teacher-directed learning and integrate the ideas of children into the framework of every lesson plan, and by doing so, they affirm children. In my work with students, I've found that a lack of intelligence is rarely a barrier to success. The main barrier is often a self-concept that is not fully developed. With affirmation, we have the opportunity to help children develop a positive self-concept.

When I say affirm children, I mean it in a very broad way. You can affirm a child, for example, by being aware of how he prefers to receive praise and acting accordingly. Chapman (1992) calls a child's preference for praise and affection his *love language*. Is he a hugger? Is he an I-want-to-hang-out-with-you kind of child? Does he feel love most clearly when you help him, when you offer him something, or when you express yourself with words? You can affirm a child by being aware of her basic personality. Is she outgoing and overt in her expressions of emotion? Is she calm and more comfortable following? Is she more comfortable when she is in control? Is she at ease when she knows all the details have been taken care of? You can affirm a child by understanding his preferred learning style and inviting him to learn that way. Does he prefer to learn in visual, auditory, or kinesthetic ways? You can affirm a child by trusting her to do something. Trust is one of the ultimate examples of affirmation. By affirming children in many ways, master teachers help young learners make connections in ways that are meaningful to them.

In the end, truly great teachers are giving the same overarching lesson every day, whether the domain of study is literacy, math, science, or social-emotional development. I like to describe the overarching lesson like this: How much do we love? Are we able to show compassion when we are not feeling compassionate? Are we able to be truthful when we are tempted otherwise? How do we behave when no one is looking over our shoulders?

I use the word *love* broadly to mean helping other people create things that, in turn, affect others positively. Someone who understands how to love and feels worthy to receive love is someone who is open to the natural energy of life itself. This kind of person is able to connect with children and adults and is at the same time passionate, yet calm in the face of that passion.

Chapter 2

. . . .

Engage All
Learning Styles

How do children learn best? How do they best connect to topics of interest? What is the most challenging way for them to learn? There are many terms in early childhood education for exploring these questions—*differentiated learning, learning styles, learning modalities,* and *learning domains,* among others. Knowing the latest terminology, however, is not the key to helping children learn. Understanding how different children learn best—understanding their natural learning styles—so we can invite all of them to become lifelong learners is what is most critical.

Some children learn best with music, others learn best using math and logic, and others prefer to be immersed in nature. The fundamental questions for us to explore as teachers include the following: How do individual children learn best within their areas of interest? In what ways can we help them improve? As an example, let's say a child feels most at home in the musical world. The question to ask is, how does this child best learn and use music? The child might be a music reader who uses sheet music, which means he is a visual learner. The child might be most comfortable learning by ear, which means she is an auditory learner. Or, the child might learn best using muscle memory, which makes him a kinesthetic learner. We'll look at these three basic styles of learning—visual, auditory, and kinesthetic—so you can identify children's preferred styles.

Engaging students in learning, of course, requires more than just categorizing them and teaching to a learning style. As an example, let's say a teacher is coaching a young baseball player who naturally bats left. She's a good batter, thinks batting is fun, builds confidence as she improves, and wants to bat more often. One day the coach introduces her to batting from the right side. It's not as easy, but with practice she becomes very good at it and becomes an even better batter in the process. Just like the coach with this developing switch-hitter in baseball, we should strive to help young children grow by inviting them into learning situations via their strengths and then challenging them to learn in other ways. Doing so helps children's brains to become quick and agile. We can help children become versatile learners with the ability to approach learning situations from different perspectives, resulting in a child who can learn in all three of the learning styles: auditory, visual, and kinesthetic.

Identify a Child's Preferred Learning Style

The three basic learning styles—visual, auditory, and kinesthetic—are not mutually exclusive, but we all tend to prefer one over the others. Our preferences often overlap and are situational. For example, I usually prefer the auditory style of learning. I learn best when I hear information aloud, and I process my emotions best when I talk about them aloud. When it comes to learning a new recipe, however, I prefer the visual and kinesthetic styles. I learn best how to prepare a meal when I see written instructions in a cookbook, watch someone else prepare it, and then experience how it feels to make a dish firsthand.

As teachers, how do we identify children's learning-style preferences? How do we use this information? To figure out how children like to learn, observe them over time. The more you observe, the more accurate your observations will be.

Auditory Learners

A child who seems unresponsive, quiet, or more willing to watch than participate is probably an auditory learner. If a child is quiet or looking away from a book being read, don't assume he isn't paying attention. He might look away or down so he's not distracted visually. As an auditory learner myself, I can share that these learners prefer to focus on what they are hearing, rather than what they are seeing. They acclimate themselves to learning through hearing. With auditory learners, the best strategy is often simply to let them be.

Visual Learners

Visual learners are sometimes mistaken for auditory learners because they also can be quiet and observant. Visual learners like to see what they are exploring and learning. If you read a book to a visual learner, for example, she will be likely to follow along on the pages as you go. In general, children who are visual learners have strong listening and observation skills.

Kinesthetic Learners

A child who touches whatever he can whenever he can probably prefers to learn kinesthetically. The next time you read to a group of children, notice which children want to touch the pictures in the book or help you turn pages. These are your kinesthetic learners. Find ways to involve these learners with touching or movement activities. Many times I'll ask a kinesthetic child to help me before he takes the initiative himself. I might offer a choice by asking a question, such as "I need someone to help me turn pages. Would you like to help?" With this simple question, I invite the kinesthetic learner to use his preferred learning style and, simultaneously, teach social-emotional skills by guiding him to be more helpful.

Learning Outside Your Comfort Zone

Using the information you gather about young children's learning styles is important and empowering for both you and the children. For the children, having their learning style honored is an open invitation to learn and play as they do best—within their comfort zone. In fact, we want children to think of *learning* and *playing* as synonyms. When a teacher only instructs in a style that is not a child's preference, the child's response is often caution and fear. Caution and fear have never produced anything of value or goodness. In contrast, when children learn and play in their preferred style, they typically respond with creativity and confidence and learn to love learning in the process. Creativity and confidence produce greatness and visionary results time and time again.

Connecting with children's learning styles is also empowering for teachers. It helps you invite children into a learning scenario where they are engaged and feel confident so that, eventually, you can challenge them to learn in ways outside their comfort zones. Not long ago, for example, I codirected a student-created musical at an elementary school in Tucson. I helped about a hundred kindergarten through fifth-grade students create an original musical based on *The Three Little Pigs*. So, really, I was codirecting thirty-five pigs, thirty trees, and thirty-five wolves, all of whom had lots of energy! For four weeks, we brainstormed the story line, wrote the script, and composed the music. Throughout this process, I asked lots of questions in ways that honored all three learning styles.

With any group of this size, some students will need a little more help than others—not because they are less intelligent, but because they are brilliant. One such student was a kindergartner named Manny, a kinesthetic learner. At the time, he was still working on his auditory and visual skills, especially the auditory skill of listening. Manny wanted to play the percussion instrument known as the claves, and my codirector, Kristy Brower, gave him the opportunity to do so. Manny excelled. His rhythm was especially impressive for such a young child. He could naturally follow the slowing and acceleration of tempo as well as keep a constant tempo. On the claves, Manny was in his comfort zone, usually smiling with joy and confidence. He ended up playing the claves for the final performance alongside the live, professional-level rhythm section. It was really a joy to see Manny play the claves and be recognized by the packed cafeteria of parents. He was beaming!

My codirector invited Manny, a strong kinesthetic learner, into the project through his strengths, and Manny became confident and engaged as a result. Importantly, and because he was engaged in the project and had master teachers to guide him, he worked on and improved his auditory skills as well, without even realizing it. As Manny played the claves, I asked if he could play softly, and he sure could—he showed me! I asked him if he could play loudly, and he did that too! Manny started playing on all sorts of things: chairs, tables, and even the back of my shoe. I wasn't concerned about what Manny was playing. Instead, I focused on finding ways for him to be his kinesthetic self while improving his auditory skills. By the day of the performance, Manny didn't need much direction from me. He used his kinesthetic strengths and improved auditory skills to know when to play loudly or softly. He also learned when playing the very loud metal chair, the somewhat loud floors and tables, and my quiet shoe made sense.

Manny also worked on his visual skills when we read the script together over and over again in those four weeks. He was engaged in the project, so reading the script was of interest to him. He improved in the area of literacy, including reading aloud, comprehension, and vocabulary. He improved in the area of math, including pattern and sequence recognition. Manny also improved his social-emotional skills, which was especially exciting because it was the area that challenged him the most.

Manny was my student, but he was also my teacher. Thank you, Manny, for reminding me to honor all learning styles and for rewarding me with that killer smile of yours.

Developing Learning Versatility

Developing learning versatility in children—developing their ability to use all three learning styles—is critical. When children grow up, they will have to sit down for long stretches of time, take notes, and be attentive listeners, which are auditory skills. They will have to read many books, which is a visual skill, and they will hopefully develop active, healthy, and fit lifestyles, which require kinesthetic skills. To use a financial metaphor, being a versatile learner is like being diversified in your investments. You want to have many resources at your disposal, not just one. Thinking about it another way, being able to learn in many ways is like being able to give and receive love in many ways: hugging, using words, and giving time and energy, among others. Successful relationships require versatility in expressing love. In sum, we want to help children learn in all three styles so they have many resources for learning and many opportunities for success. Like anything else, it is much easier for people to learn these skills as children—when they are, by default, living like a child—than as adults.

Teachers who honor all three learning styles use creative tools and variations to help children absorb content and concepts while also developing other learning styles, just as Manny's teachers did in the earlier example. This level of teaching doesn't require a long-term project. Reciting or singing a rhyme or song, for example, can involve saying the words aloud (auditory skill), seeing the words of the lyrics as they're being spoken (visual skill), and beating the cadence of the rhyme with one's hands (kinesthetic skill).

As another example, think about The Tree and the Wind activity (page 104)—a game in which teachers and children become full-bodied trees, complete with moving branches that respond to the wind and rain. How is each learner invited into the activity? How might a master teacher encourage the development of other skills and knowledge? Kinesthetic children are invited through movement as their bodies become the trees, branches, and leaves and as their breath becomes the wind, rain, snow, and other components of the weather. Their bodies and voices become the birds, squirrels, and other animals that visit the trees. These children use their bodies as they learn how to predict weather systems, classify animals, and explore what kinds of trees live in different environments. They use their bodies as they expand their vocabulary and increase their comprehension skills. They use their bodies as they play with their peers and develop social-emotional skills. By playing this game kinesthetically, these children are learning in a way that is meaningful to them and are given the opportunity to use their strengths to explore other topics and learning styles along the way.

The teacher engages visual learners in The Tree and the Wind game by inviting them to watch their fellow classmates. These learners gain knowledge as they watch others act like trees. Everyone is doing something different, something unique. The teacher leads with words and encourages sounds—promoting auditory-skill development—but also leads with visually stimulating movements. When visual learners imagine their fingers as leaves and pretend the leaves are falling off the tree and blowing in the wind, they learn about scientific concepts such as gravity, wind, and seasons. Invited to the activity visually, these children are also introduced to kinesthetic and auditory styles of learning.

The teacher invites auditory learners to play The Tree and the Wind game through sounds of voices and early classical music. These learners may not move as much or as gracefully as the kinesthetic learners, but they are learning nevertheless. They listen to the sounds of nature, including the sound of the rain that grows from sprinkles to a full thunderstorm, being made by the other children's voices. These learners hear the sound of a bird visiting a tree and might explore the concept of perspective—how the sound changes as the bird gets closer or farther away, softer then louder. These learners are encouraged if the teacher's voice is enthusiastic; using different timbres can help keep these learners interested as they explore.

Similarly, when you play the Surfing the Words game (page 146) with children, you can change the volume, pace, and inflection of your voice to match the volume, pace, and inflection of the music and story so that auditory learners are immersed in a world they understand and love. You can use the images and words of the book to stimulate the interest of the visual learners. You can engage kinesthetic learners by inviting them to become the actions and characters in the book—a rainstorm, a wave crashing down on a beach, a dancing giraffe, a howling wolf, or a porcupine who thinks she is fluffy. Reading to young children doesn't have to be a quiet activity; it often can be more effective as an active, high-energy time.

Variations within Learning Styles

All learners are different. In other words, identifying how a child learns is not a multiple-choice test with only three or four answers. Not all visual learners are the same, nor are all auditory learners or all kinesthetic learners.

An auditory learner who has a strong second preference for visual learning but a weak preference for kinesthetic learning is very different from an auditory learner who has a strong second preference for kinesthetic learning but a weak preference for visual learning. Think about the first child in this example, the strong auditory learner who also likes to learn visually but not kinesthetically. If you were reading to this child, she would likely sit still and watch and listen very carefully. Now think about the second child in this example, the strong auditory learner who also likes to learn kinesthetically but not visually. If you were reading to this child, he would be interested in what you were saying, but might not hold constant eye contact on the book. He would likely alternate from sitting still to moving around like a character in the book.

A master teacher might change the pace of a reading activity by alternating between reading and discussing a story to becoming the characters of the story with movement. This master teacher would still be teaching literacy social-emotional skills with the story, but would also be engaging the children in all three learning styles. All of the children's interests would be captured, which leads to more self-regulation, deeper learning, and more joyful learning. Joyful learning experiences help create lifelong learners.

If I were to assign a number from one to five to children's learning preferences, a small classroom sample might look like this:

	Auditory	Kinesthetic	Visual
Child 1	3	5	1
Child 2	1	3	5
Child 3	5	1	3
Child 4	2	4	3
Child 5	4	2	1

Key

1 = extremely strong   2 = strong   3 = average
4 = weak   5 = extremely weak

This table utilizes a very simple scale to illustrate a point, but actual variations are far more complex than what can be shown on a five-point scale. Even further, this example doesn't account for the child who prefers two learning styles equally. The list of learning preferences in any classroom will be diverse, and the degree of variations complex.

For these reasons, the Life Learning Techniques described in part 2 of this book, honor this Master Teaching Principle and engage all learning styles. In doing so, the techniques invite young children to learn and grow, giving them authentic—not artificial—reasons for wanting to learn. Honoring the learning styles helps children find within themselves the voice that says, "I want to learn," "I love to learn," and "I want to achieve." Once children experience this personal paradigm shift, they will find new opportunities for learning they never new existed. Learning becomes a lifestyle, and it becomes easy; or rather, the hard work needed becomes easier because the work is part of quenching the thirst for learning.

By keeping this Master Teaching Principle in mind as we guide children, we greatly increase our chance of turning our youngest learners into future thinkers and creators. Honor the three basic learning styles, invite children to explore and learn, and watch our next generation of young adults excel.

Chapter 3

. . . .

Ask Questions to Develop Critical-Thinking Skills

Take a moment and visualize yourself playing outside with a child. You feel a warm autumn breeze and see leaves falling from trees to the ground. The leaves are different colors, and you, the master teacher, ask the child, "Why do leaves fall?" "Why do the leaves fall so slowly?" "Why are the leaves different colors?" or "Why don't the leaves fall in a straight line?" After you ask, you *listen* to the child's response, which means you don't talk. You are careful not to overload. You take cues from the child about what topic or idea to discuss next.

A master teacher does more than present knowledge to be absorbed by students. A master teacher uses questions to feed a child's natural curiosity and uses the child's answers to know when to switch gears. Questions allow teachers to guide a topic in many ways, connecting the topic to different personalities, love languages, and learning styles.

This process of asking questions and then looking for more possibilities has a name, which I picked up from my mentor and friend Mimi Brodsky Chenfeld. It's called *What else?* This approach helps us create new knowledge, build on that knowledge, and then use that knowledge in empowering ways; it has served many leaders and creative individuals. Can we use this approach with young children in our preschool

classrooms, elementary schools, and homes? Absolutely. Ask questions
and see where they lead.

Conversing with Children

We must continually remind ourselves to ask children questions. When
I say "ask questions," I mean it in a very broad way:

- Ask questions using words.

- Use body language to ask a question.

- Use a picture to pose a question.

- Ask linear questions.

- Ask abstract questions.

- Present questions that lead to deductive reasoning.

Questions engage thinking skills. When all children have to do is fill in
a box or choose from multiple-choice answers, much less thinking is
going on.

I have met adults who don't think children are capable of having
conversations with adults. I have met adults who think children should
play and converse only with children, and adults should have discussions only with other adults. This kind of thinking is outdated and,
more to the point, arrogant. A lot of social-emotional development
occurs when children play with their peers, but time with adults is
important too—for everyone involved. I have had some amazing conversations with young children. Children are experts at imagination,
and some children understand things like art and creativity better than
many adults. The next time you're with a young child, get crazy, live on
the edge, and ask, "How are you?" See where it takes you.

When asking children questions to engage their imagination,
remember the following:

- Ask open-ended questions.

- Be patient, quiet, and inviting.

- Allow children to answer and engage you in an actual conversation.

For some adults, this is a pretty tall order because asking a four-year-old a question means that we have to stop talking, stop giving directions, and stop controlling. It means we have to take time to actually listen. The reward is a real conversation with that four-year-old and great fun.

Asking open-ended questions that engage children's interest is, perhaps, the most critical point. To practice using open-ended questions to help children think critically and deductively, play The Tree and the Wind (page 104) with them. When young children are allowed the time to ponder and think for themselves, they will begin to utilize some of the critical Life Learning Techniques—such as imagination, visualization, and affirmation—discussed in part 2.

Sometimes teachers ask me how I deal with discipline challenges in the classroom while also fostering creativity. Disciplinary action is sometimes unavoidable, but many discipline problems can be prevented entirely. I've found that disruptive behaviors often occur because a child is not interested or engaged in an activity. If you keep children engaged, you'll have fewer discipline problems; one of the best ways to keep children engaged is to ask questions.

Asking Questions to Nurture Creativity

Asking questions and creativity are two partners on the same path. For creativity to flourish, questions must be asked. Children are naturally full of questions. I'm sure you know more than one child who asks, "Why?" multiple times during a day. If a child approaches you during any activity and asks, "Why are you doing that?" you could respond by asking, "Why do you think I am?" See how the child responds. Inviting children to answer their own "Why?" questions is a powerful way to help them learn to think in depth in any situation.

Some questions are asked and explored silently. If a child is intently playing with a toy or repeatedly opening and closing a door, she is likely asking herself questions about how something works or looking for patterns or sequences. If you see a child playing a game or struggling with some activity, you might suggest how he can enjoy the game even more, and then ask questions or wait for the child to ask questions as he tries a new way. Sometimes a question might not seem to have the desired effect, but a question always results in some reaction and some level of critical thinking in the child's mind, whether or not it's apparent. Asking questions can open a door for children, nudging them into a realm of creativity.

Using Questions to Create Student Musicals

I have the pleasure of working on four student-created musicals each year with my codirector, Kristy Brower. The four musicals are created by children—preschool through fifth grade—in groups organized by reading level. In brainstorming sessions guided by Kristy and me, the children develop the story line and the script themselves. These sessions involve asking lots of questions, and boy do the kids have answers!

In the summer of 2009, we guided about a hundred children (kindergarten through fifth-grade students) in developing an original musical based on *The Three Little Pigs*. We posed many questions, including "Why is the Big, Bad Wolf so mean?" The answers flowed in with excited facial expressions and energized body movements. The children became many of the descriptive words they offered as answers. One answer was, "He's a bully," to which we asked, "Why is he a bully?" The responses were diverse: "He's jealous of how happy the pigs are," "He's sad about something," and "He's scared about something." A second-grade student spoke up and said, "I think the other wolves are getting tired of being bossed around by the Big, Bad Wolf." We kept asking the kids questions, and eventually they decided that one of the wolves in the pack was a vegetarian, but that he had kept it a secret. That's right, a closet vegetarian wolf! This wolf's dilemma worked itself into a song called the "Big, Bad Wolf Blues":

> We like to eat meat.
> We do not eat ham.
> But one of our brothers
> Is a vegetarian!

You get the picture. Lots of questions helped encourage in-depth and abstract thinking about character development, the script, and the music. The students all had a fantastic time, learned a great deal, and created an original and exciting musical they were proud of. At the core of this process was the asking of questions.

At this same school, I also worked with fourth and fifth graders to create an original production of *Snow White and the Seven Dwarfs*. We asked hundreds of questions. Some were general, such as "What do you want this musical to be like?" and others were more specific. One of the ideas that emerged in brainstorming was to change the names of the dwarfs. One boy said, "Can we name one of the dwarfs Gordo?" This common Spanish nickname means fat or chubby and is used as a term of endearment. The students ended up changing the names of all the dwarfs, some of which were simply "kid funny," for example, Stinky and Picky.

Later in the process, we asked the question, "Why is the queen so mean?" The words *greedy* and *jealous* came up. My codirector and I then introduced the word *vain*. We then became the word with our bodies and faces to make sure all learning styles were engaged. The students, Kristy, and I then agreed that the queen needed a song. I asked the question, "What would a vain and greedy queen sing?" A bubbly child popped out of her chair and said, "I know! I know!" She sauntered to the side of the classroom, struck a flamenco pose, and exclaimed,

"She'd say, 'It's me, it's me, it's all about me!'" Kristy typed the words onto the interactive whiteboard while I asked the children how the melody should make us all feel. I scribbled the melody in C minor with the children's words as lyrics. The result was a fabulous tango!

Because the fourth and fifth graders were actively involved and engaged in the creative process, the entire journey was meaningful to them. Months later, students were still coming up to me and saying, "We still talk about that show!" Questions were the springboard to critical thinking and creativity. At the same time, children learned how to set goals, work toward them, and produce a result. The project built students' self-concept as evidenced in their confidence in approaching, speaking, and interacting with others as the musical developed. Additionally, many students improved their reading and comprehension skills while working on the script, which was fantastic. The students were absolutely beaming with pride at the end of the process. And at the core of it all? Questions.

Not every question works perfectly. That's okay. Explore with children and use questions as the starting point to truly meaningful learning. Combine asking questions with improvising and you have the makings of a master teacher!

Chapter 4

• • • • • • • • • • •

Improvise to Encourage Creativity

In a world where we assess only results and not process, teachers can feel as if there is little room for improvisation. Ironically, when teachers become truly great at improvising, they teach the most important thing any student can learn—how to create and how to be creative. We are built to create, and we create many things, such as ideas, solutions to problems, and art.

Let's start by breaking down something teachers are familiar with: lesson plans. Some educators claim that lesson plans are extremely important. Others claim that they are highly overrated. Both statements are somewhat true. As my brother Ted once said, "The truth often lies somewhere in between." Lesson plans are meant to be guides but nothing more. In other words, a lesson plan is a great tool as long as the plan is not an end but, rather, one means to an end. A plan should not dictate the learning process; it should be a flexible framework that is revised and reworked based on children's input, learning styles, and interests. Even though learning is the goal of every lesson, the specific path a teacher follows to achieve that goal will sometimes need change.

The most successful people know when to follow structure and rules and when to go beyond them; that is, they don't hold to a rule or structure, such as a lesson plan, without evaluating whether it makes sense to do so. People who only follow the rules, while certainly able to live meaningful and loving lives, are not leaders of change. Similarly, an audience is rarely, if ever, inspired by scripted sets of information that don't allow for change.

Improvisation is one of the most critical components to the art of guiding others. You must adapt and improvise to work with different learners. In order to improvise successfully, you must connect with others so you know who they are and how to guide them. At the same time, to inspire and lead you must share who you are with children. Connecting emotionally leads to trust, which gives both the teacher and students the confidence needed to improvise, allowing everyone to reach new heights.

Having a strong grasp of content is also important for improvisation. Your knowledge of the content must be so deep that you can focus on *how* you are teaching rather than on *what* you are teaching. You also must always keep in mind *why* you are teaching. Remembering why you teach is the best of all motivators. It will give you the internal fortitude, patience, and perseverance to try different ways to help children make connections for understanding. If you know why you teach, others will follow you, young children will flock to you, learning opportunities will be plentiful, and your work will be fulfilling.

Improvisation in Action

One of my most memorable experiences with improvisation took place when I was playing The Tree and the Wind (page 104) with a group of about fifty energetic three-, four-, and five-year-olds in Akron, Ohio. The children and I were pretending to be trees and were creating the sound of rain with basic breathing techniques. We were breathing in through our noses and out through our mouths, making the *shh* sound of the rain. We moved our arms high above our heads and then low to our stomachs as our branches moved in the wind. Everyone was "in the moment" of being a tree—drinking rain, becoming stronger, and enjoying the company of fellow trees.

And then it happened. Pepito screamed, "My tree got cut down!" and fell to the floor. Almost immediately, half of the trees decided they had been cut down as well. In a split second, I went from having a forest of breathing, moving trees to having twenty-five dead trees—and they were not-moving-sprawled-out-on-the-floor dead. In addition, I had twenty-five alive but very confused trees. I had about three seconds to make a decision. I could either (a) tell the dead trees to stop being dead trees or (b) somehow use the dead-tree scenario as a learning opportunity. Intuitively, I chose b.

I decided to become a cut-down tree as well, which inspired the remaining trees to fall into dead-tree land as well. It was a very relaxing place! So there we were, fifty dead trees. What I failed to mention earlier is that a group of parents and teachers were in the back of the room observing, stifling their giggles, and probably thinking, "Now what are you going to do?" At that moment, I asked a question in my best dead-tree voice, "What do dead trees need to grow?" Pepito answered in a magnificent, creaky, and old-sounding dead-tree voice, "Raaaaaain." It was the same answer I often got when I asked this question of the living trees. We all began to breathe in through our noses and out through our mouths, creating sounds of the rain. We slowly began to grow again until we were standing.

It was at that wonderful moment that I began to talk about the circle of life. Then, in the middle of the conversation, Pepito yelled, "My tree got cut down again!" Needless to say, we experienced the circle of life numerous times that day, but I was ready to improvise at any moment. The children learned something new that day, practiced breathing exercises, moved their bodies, and used creativity—all because of play-based teaching and improvisation.

Before you are too impressed with my improvisation skills, know that The Tree and the Wind game was designed to help teachers improvise. The game is set up like a template; there is no single way to play it. When Pepito and I improvised, we were really just playing the game. Does any game or lesson always go smoothly? No. Change is one of the few constants.

As an example, one afternoon I was playing The Tree and the Wind with a four-year-old who was having a tough day. His bad mood was not noticeable at first. All the children, except this one little boy, were participating in the game and breathing over and over again to the soothing sound of rain. After a while, the boy said to me in a soft but annoyed voice, "I don't want to be a tree." Wearing my improvisation hat, I quickly replied, "That's okay. You don't have to be a tree. You can watch if you'd like." This tactic usually works, but it didn't this time. As the other preschoolers breathed and visualized birds of different colors visiting their trees, the boy approached me again and said in a soft and more agitated voice, "I don't like trees."

This response was new to me. I had never met a young child who did not like trees. I responded by saying, "It's all right. You don't have to be a tree. You know, you can be a forest ranger and drive a truck through the forest to make sure there aren't any fires." I thought my improvisation was pretty amazing, but the boy did not. He was not interested in this idea. Even worse, his agitation level was higher than ever. He started to shake in anger, and then he screamed, "I . . . *(deep, quick breathing)* hate . . . *(more breathing)* treeeeeeeees!" The scream zapped all the energy in the room.

I didn't know what to do, so I did the only think I could think of: I asked him an open-ended question, "What do you want to be?" His body language changed from expressing anger to expressing excitement. He smiled and said, "Spido-Man!" otherwise known as Spider-Man. I responded very seriously, "That's a great idea." I stuck my hand out to form a famous Spider-Man pose. I took a deep breath through my nose and hissed it out through my mouth as I poured a massive amount of pretend spiderwebs across the classroom.

This action was met with great joy by all the children. We were now playing Spider-Man. Once the children were engaged in the game, I said, "My name is Enrique, and the first letter in my name is *E*. Let's make the letter *E* with spiderwebs!" Everyone joined this visualization exercise. Just when I thought it couldn't get any better, a little girl said in a squeaky, bright voice, "My . . . my . . . my letter is *A*." She smiled. I knew what she expected. We all made the letter *A* with spiderwebs. In the end, we made everyone's letter with spiderwebs. Improvising led us to even more breathing and visualizing, and it led us to practicing literacy skills.

How many versions of a game are there? I don't know. Each game is different each time I play it with children, in the same way a lesson is different each time I teach it to children. I encourage you to make every game and idea in this book your own. Improvise and make changes that will help you connect with the children in your life.

Bring Your Brain to Class

Know your content and have a lesson plan, but remember to bring your brain to class every day and to really listen to children's ideas. Listen to what children are saying both verbally and nonverbally. Pay attention to the cues they give you with their interests, learning styles, and answers to your questions.

Improvising is a lot like many things done at a high level. Great chefs must improvise to solve problems in the kitchen. Great athletes must improvise during a sporting event to make great plays. Musicians must be able to improvise to reach great heights. Entrepreneurs must improvise as business plans change. Skillful teachers and parents are no exception. Plan and hope for the future, but live and improvise in the moment.

Chapter 5

· · · · · · · · · · ·

Teach and Learn
in Width and Depth

In addition to honoring our mentors, engaging all learning styles, asking questions, and improvising, master teachers approach teaching in *width* and *depth*. Learning in width and depth is distinct from linear and abstract learning. In fact, you can learn in depth and width in both linear and abstract ways. Students of any learning style can learn a topic with width or depth. While both kinds of learning are important, learning in depth offers more of an intellectual challenge and is related to higher brain functioning. Examples of learning in width and depth follow.

Learning in Width

Learning in width means learning in broad strokes and looking at multiple topics but not exploring any one topic deeply. This may sound like something a teacher should avoid, but learning in width is important because it gives students a bird's-eye view of a topic. For example, let's say you are teaching a class on the American Revolution and are approaching it with width. You'd cover many of the major events of the revolution, and your lesson would probably follow a time line that would look something like this:

1754–63	French and Indian War
1764	Sugar Act
1765	Patrick Henry's "If This Be Treason" speech
1770	Boston Massacre
1773	Boston Tea Party
1775	Paul Revere's ride and the "shot heard around the world"
1775	Battle of Bunker Hill
1776	Declaration of Independence
1778	French Alliance
1779	Spain's declaration of war on Great Britain
1781	Articles of Confederation ratified
1783	Treaty of Paris
1787	Signing of the US Constitution
1788	US Constitution ratified

Looking at this historical period in width helps students understand the scope of the American Revolution and the sequence of events. Students can then put together the pieces like a puzzle.

Let's say you are teaching a preschool class about letters and their sounds. Learning in width might look something like this:

- singing the alphabet song

- reading picture or alphabet books that discuss the first letter of words

- learning the basic sounds of letters

- using movement to become letters and groups of letters

- drawing letters in the air with breathing games

Learning in width has a purpose, but if you teach only in width, children will not understand how concepts fit together. Understanding why certain actions caused particular consequences and understanding how letters interact to form words requires a different kind of learning. It requires looking at a topic in depth.

Learning in Depth

Learning in depth means exploring the details of a topic and looking at the topic from different perspectives. Learning in depth helps learners make connections within a single topic. This kind of learning, delivered in interesting ways, creates lasting and meaningful learning experiences. Going back to the American Revolution example, learning in depth might involve selecting one of the events from the time line and looking at it in detail.

For example, if you chose to look at the French and Indian War (1754–63) in depth, you might discover the following: The conflict was serious and involved multiple countries. *French and Indian War* was the term used in the colonies for the part of the war fought in North America; the larger war involved Austria, France, Great Britain, Prussia, and Sweden. Events took place in North America, the West Indies, Europe, and even India. France, with the help of its allies Sweden and Austria, fought against Frederick the Great of Prussia in Europe. The English and French fought for control of the colonies in North America, the West Indies, and India. The English won control of the North American colonies, but the cost was huge, putting Great Britain in debt. To pay this debt, Great Britain taxed the colonies excessively. These taxes and a number of other factors eventually led to the Revolutionary War a decade later. So the French and Indian War was one of the causes of the American Revolution.

Learning in depth with preschool students who are studying letters might involve taking the letters and playing with them in combinations. Over time, children will begin to understand that letters make sounds on their own and also in combination. For example, let's say you have a preschool student named Tania. She learns the *T* sound when you teach in width. To teach in depth, you might explore what sound the letter *T* makes when combined with other letters. Tania might begin to explore how the other letters in her name combine, such as how *T* works with *A*. She then might explore how *T* sounds when it is next to an *H*, such as in the word *that*. By learning in depth, Tania will discover that the letter *T* has many uses and combines with other letters in many ways. As with all learning, these discoveries are best encouraged in play-based ways.

Connecting Width and Depth

Teaching in depth is certainly important, but teaching in width is important too. Master teachers encourage learning in width and depth simultaneously, helping children make connections along the way. Masterful learning occurs when knowledge is both wide and deep. To encourage learning in depth, master teachers find different ways to say the same thing. While doing so, they may end up following many tangents that support the topic in depth. These tangents will likely lead to new topics, which then creates more width. An opposite approach to teaching and learning would be a "buffet approach," or picking and choosing specific things to learn but not connecting the elements in depth. A buffet approach may be appropriate sometimes, but it's not appropriate as a systemic approach to education.

Let's think about these approaches another way. Consider a very simple meal, such as a homemade grilled hamburger on a fresh bun with crisp lettuce, ripe tomatoes, mustard, and ketchup. The ingredients come together as you taste them, and the burger is simple yet delicious. You have width in the burger because you have a number of ingredients you can see clearly. There are few opportunities for the ingredients' flavors to meld. You know exactly what you're tasting. That is an example of a meal in width. Now consider dining at a fine restaurant that uses fresh ingredients and sees food as an art form. You eat several courses, and each one combines many herbs, sauces, and other ingredients that meld together to create new flavors. This is an example of a meal that has a lot of depth. In tasting these melded flavors, you could try to figure out the dish's width—the specific ingredients that created the combination. You also could choose just to enjoy its depth—the combined flavors and various textures that surprise your mouth and taste buds. Experiencing a meal in depth transcends the experience of simply eating.

In most cases, you need to master the fundamentals before you can learn in depth. But ultimately you need to learn in both width and depth to really understand any subject. You can use the other Master Teaching Principles to help you teach in both width and depth. You can ask questions and remember the power of the one-word question *why*. If you are playing a game involving a puppet, for example, and the children identify the puppet's emotion, don't stop there. Ask, "Why does the puppet feel sad?" and "What could have happened to make him sad?" Then wait, give children time to think, and then listen—which you might find difficult at first. In today's world, we can be so focused on the answer that we forget why the answer is even important. The process of exploring a question to get to an answer—or answers—is a valuable and affirming learning experience.

Digging Deep within Ourselves

One of my most memorable experiences with learning in width and depth took place during a tuba lesson with Fritz Kaenzig at the University of Illinois at Urbana–Champaign. It was my first lesson as a master's student, and even though I knew Fritz's reputation as a great teacher, I did not realize how much he was going to teach me and expect from me. Fritz was interested in helping me create music at the highest level I possibly could. Fritz knew I was a top dog throughout high school and my undergraduate years, and he knew I was passionate and driven. I had experienced learning in width and depth before, but I had no idea how much more depth there was to learn.

Because I didn't know Fritz yet, I thought I was just going to take a lesson. I was very prepared. I brought in a set of Schubert songs I had already published myself. I played with dynamics, with phrasing gestures, and with all the tempo markings. I didn't miss a note. When I was done, I put down my tuba and waited for what I was used to receiving—praise. After all, I had performed well in width (in the technical preparation of the music) and even somewhat well in depth (with the phrasing, gestures, and so on).

Instead of praise, I was met with silence, which lasted for about thirty seconds, though it felt much longer. The silence was punctuated by a pensive, yet tense, stare from Fritz. He tilted his head and placed his hand near his chin as he looked at me. He thought and thought and then looked at me and then thought some more. Finally, he said, "Is that all you have to say?" He didn't scream, and he wasn't nasty. He went on to say that he expected more from me and that he was not impressed. I left that first lesson quietly, but I was very angry and silently weeping— not the kind of weeping that occurs when you are hurt physically, but the kind that makes you want to put your fist through a wall.

I practiced that week more than I had ever practiced in my life, even though I was busier than ever as a graduate assistant for the band program. Not only did I practice, but I practiced differently. I looked for the deeper meaning in the Schubert songs I was performing. What were the songs really saying? What was the composer going through in that time in his life? How could I express myself and my experiences through this music? I came to my next lesson inspired and driven to create great music. I did, and Fritz smiled.

During the first lesson, Fritz improvised, not with harmony or rhythm, but with my psyche. Fritz took someone who was used to learning in width on a journey of educational depth. It was not enough to have all the right notes, dynamics, phrasing, and tempo markings. Fritz wanted to know what I was trying to say musically, emotionally, and spiritually. He dug down deep into me and, more importantly, asked me to dig deeper within myself. I dug in, and I thought deeply about what I wanted to convey with music. Later in life, I continued to dig deeply, asking myself why I was teaching.

My first lesson with Fritz is a great example of how to balance depth and width while teaching. Would you want to stare down four-year-olds to push them further? Of course not! Balancing width and depth will look different in the early childhood world. Think about reading to a group of children. You might start by teaching in width: reading a book once and then moving on to another book. If the children love a particular book, however, you'll likely read it numerous times and add something new each time. You might have the children draw their favorite character in the book to keep them engaged and then talk about how that character feels and why. You might read the book with music in the background. You might have the children act out the scenes. You could have the children experience the book in many ways. Teaching one book in many ways is an example of teaching young children in depth. To balance width and depth, read a variety of books for width, but also choose to experience each book in various auditory, kinesthetic, and visual ways for depth.

Approaching Each Lesson as a Unique Opportunity

Here's another example of teaching in width and depth simultaneously. I once heard a fantastic voice teacher working with a very talented young woman. She already had great pitch, rhythm, and more, but the teacher knew she had much more potential. She hadn't taken flight with her voice yet; she hadn't consistently let her voice truly soar, especially as a soloist. Did he approach each lesson like every other lesson? No. He approached each lesson as a unique opportunity and was not stifled by traditional approaches of repetition.

In this particular instance, he chose to teach this student in depth based on something she already knew; he added movement to her breathing as she approached the apex of a phrase. As the student sang higher and higher, almost reaching the highest note in a song, he asked her to bend her knees. This technique helped her release her breath and her song. (In part 2 of this book, you'll learn how to use this idea with young children.) This outstanding teacher, who was on his way to becoming a master teacher, used the trust he had built with this student over the preceding year to help her take flight. Her voice soared.

Each lesson offers unique opportunities for learning, especially if we are open and looking for them. Let's say you are talking with a group of five-year-olds about a recently watched DVD. You hear a child use the word *exciting*. At that moment, you have an opportunity to take a word the children already know, *exciting*, and introduce them to other words that have a similar meaning, thus expanding their vocabulary. Words such as *thrilling*, *fantastic*, and *incredible* could and should be introduced. Having a running list of synonyms in your head or, even better, written out so that the children can see them is a tip I often share with teachers.

Teaching the Same Thing Different Ways

I studied tuba for six years with one of the finest brass teachers in the world, Dan Perantoni. Dan used many techniques to teach the same thing. He improvised until I had a deep understanding of how to do something myself. He asked many questions and made me think. He also taught in width and depth and used different learning styles until he found an approach that worked for the specific skill he was teaching.

Once while I was studying a piece of music by the German composer Richard Wagner, Dan tried to teach me the difference between the French and German styles of accent. (An accent is a note that you stress more than others, making the articulation of the note crisper.) He compared the accent in the Wagner piece to the accent in a piece by French composer Hector Berlioz. He tried many ways to explain the difference in accents to me. He used words to describe it. He demonstrated it for me. He used some breathing-related strategies. Even after all of this, I still couldn't conceptualize what he was explaining. Nothing changed how I approached the accent in French and German compositions.

Then he asked me to put down my tuba. He slapped his thighs with his hands, once lightly and once with more force. He then repeated this action on my thighs. Finally, I understood the difference between the accents. Using a kinesthetic learning style—while simultaneously improvising and teaching in depth— Dan had me *experience* the difference between Germanic and French accents. Dan was and still is a magician at teaching the same thing in many ways until he finds a path that works for each student's style of learning. Did he also teach in width by covering numerous brass fundamentals? Of course. But he also taught a deeper context so that the understanding of any technique was connected to the concept of making and creating music.

Being able to say or teach the same thing in many ways is just as important when working with young children. Sharing, for example, is a concept that often challenges young children. I approach this topic over and over again and use different approaches each time to help them to see sharing as a positive thing. I usually begin by asking a simple question, such as "Would you like to share that toy with Lisa?" You never know. The child might like to share! Many times, though, this simple question does not work, so I try to find another way to present the idea of sharing. I might say, "Would you like to share the toy or the book with Lisa?" or "Would you like to help Lisa?" or "How could we help Lisa feel happy?" I do not ask all these questions at the same time, of course. Too many questions at once would feel like an interrogation and would not be a very good idea. Using these questions over time, however, eventually works. Asking questions also helps adults practice teaching many ways.

Teaching in Width and Depth Simultaneously

My daughter Samantha loves soccer and has played for a number of years. A friend of mine once told me that great dads take interest in their child's interests, so I volunteered as a youth soccer coach. About two years into my coaching experience, I met Mark Francis, the director of coaching at the Fort Lowell Soccer Club in Tucson, Arizona. He suggested I pursue a National "D" License in soccer coaching, so I did. I spent two weekends playing soccer and having my soccer skills assessed. It was challenging, but I learned a lot about the game. Topics of width, such as the rules and basic strategies of soccer, made up about half of what I learned. Topics of depth, such as how to help young players see the field and work on techniques simultaneously, made up the other half.

Mark, originally from Trinidad, became a mentor for me in my six years of coaching soccer. He teaches with a sense of joy and is a master at using simple games and questions to refocus the energy of young athletes. He also is amazing to watch as he teaches in width and depth at the same time. His soccer practices flow with seamless transitions. He trains players while simultaneously having a great time and helping them go with the flow in the moment of a play.

Most of the time, Mark sits quietly and watches and observes so that he can guide at the most appropriate time. He often takes one soccer-related game—one template—and uses it to teach many things. For example, when he is teaching how to receive a soccer ball, he will use a particular soccer-related game but will change the parameters of that game over time so that the children are also working on spacing. To anyone on the sidelines, the game looks the same as it always has, but it isn't. It's an extension of the last game and an example of teaching in width and depth simultaneously.

You can practice teaching in width and depth simultaneously with The Tree and the Wind game (page 104). In the game, children imagine that their bodies are trees as they breathe deeply to improve and grow in many areas. While the children are making the sound of rain, breathing in through their noses and out through their mouths, you could guide them to explore the domain of science and nature by asking questions, such as "What kinds of animals live in trees?" or "Why do leaves fall off trees?" or "What happens to the rain if it gets really cold? While the children are rhythmically breathing (learning in width), they are also exploring many facts related to seasons and predicting natural occurrences (learning in depth).

Balancing Width and Depth for Effective Learning

Of course, many other opportunities in the early childhood world lead to learning in width and depth. In chapter 4, for example, I told the story about Pepito, the boy who yelled out "My tree got cut down!" during The Tree and the Wind game, which led to a class exploration of the circle of life (page 38). Pepito was thinking like a master teacher. He took the width of the game—becoming a tree and making the sound of rain—and used it to explore depth within the game—going off-script and improvising a new ending. Pepito was thinking in both linear and abstract ways, and he was thinking creatively based on what he knew and where he could go within the framework of the game. As far as I could tell, he was doing all of this intuitively. This is another example of the power of living like a child.

Pepito was thinking like Julius Shulman, a great photographer of Californian modernist architecture. Shulman knew that the camera was the least important thing about being a photographer; inspiration and the picture in the mind's eye were far more important. For Pepito, the game itself was less important than the possibilities the game offered. Pepito was also acting like the great Olympic athletes who transcend sport and constantly improvise to react and create an advantage. Pepito was doing what many children do—living in the moment and committing all his energy to it. Pepito reminds us, as teachers, to find that same energy and level of connection within ourselves.

Width and depth are two sides of the same coin. For learning to be multidimensional and effective, width and depth must be balanced.

Affirming young children has been a popular topic for many years because children who have a strong sense of self and who feel they can accomplish anything are children who are willing to take the risks necessary to create. The empowered child will take full advantage of the techniques used by teachers. A Head Start teacher in Coshocton, Ohio, explains it this way:

> These techniques have helped me adjust to the stress in my life. They also have given me new ways to introduce activities in the classroom. I use many of these techniques with my class. The children have realized that they can be champions regardless of their background.

Affirmation is the foundation to all learning. Without it, much of a child's energy will be spent attempting to be accepted. Children with a strong self-concept spend their energy exploring and creating.

Breathe and Relax

The Life Learning Techniques are meant to help adults and children live with a relaxed body and an alert mind. Living this way helps us all deal with stress. Teaching young children how to be calm, how to remain calm in stressful situations, and how to be calm as a way of living will change their lives and the lives of those around them. This state of mind and body allows us to live in the moment—just *being*— and commit all that we are to whatever we are focused on—just *doing.* Doing is what happens when we are comfortable with being. Our actions—doing—are connected to our ability to be.

Breathing deeply and smoothly is a cornerstone of having a relaxed body and alert mind. Breathing deeply impacts how energy moves in the body, and it directly affects how relaxed and focused we feel. By breathing deeply and slowly, we can even lower our heart rates. Scientific research has shown that the lower our heart rates, the faster our minds can function—this is one more reason why including deep breathing into your everyday routine with children is important.

Tammy Prado, another Head Start teacher, describes how she uses breathing techniques with other teachers and with children:

> We [the teachers] breathe every morning before the children come in. I really feel this calms us and helps us get through the day. We do the breathing with the children before circle time and when they are getting ready for naptime. The children really like deep breathing. We even hang things from the ceiling so children can have something to blow on. My self-esteem as a teacher has bloomed!

The Life Learning Techniques are as effective with adults as with children. You might encourage parents to use the same breathing and relaxation techniques at home. A parent in Athens, Ohio, reports the following:

> In my personal life and as a single mother of three, I find myself using the techniques to calm myself and to help relieve stress. I even have my son breathing and relaxing and learning to take a minute to think before he reacts.

If educators involve parents in teaching children to be relaxed and focused, they could certainly impact the overall education of children worldwide. Taking time to simply be and breathe, to appreciate the simple pleasures of life, and to recognize the beauty around us is not only relaxing but healthy and related to having longer and more fulfilling lives.

IMAGINE OR VISUALIZE

I encourage young children to visualize a new idea or a self-affirming thought every day. I might say, "Pretend you're an eagle that is flying in the sky. What do you see?" or "Step onto a cloud and feel it lift you high into the air. How is the weather?" or "What do you want to be when you're bigger or older?"

One parent explains how she and her daughter visualize:

> My daughter is very athletic, and I am attempting to teach her to relax and breathe before her games and to visualize her role as a team member.

Visualizing, using your mind to see things before they happen or to see how things could be, is a technique that has been employed by successful people throughout history. In the field of early childhood education, synonyms for *visualize* are *use your imagination* and sometimes *pretend*.

MOVE

Children love to move, and their natural energy and curiosity make movement an important part of their daily routine. An hour of movement might be all that is needed for one child, but another child might need movement most of the time. As guides, we can either attempt to control children's natural energy, or we can find ways to use it as a learning vehicle.

When teachers integrate movement into learning moments at various times throughout the day, discipline challenges seem to evaporate. Using movement-based games as a bridge to learning doesn't mean the children are jumping and skipping all day long. Nevertheless, by embracing a child's natural need to move, teachers can help children release their energy. A lot can be learned during this release of energy. For example, I sometimes ask children what letters they can spell with their bodies while lying down on the ground. Not only does this activity involve movement and literacy, it also encourages visualization. I use many dance and movement activities that involve becoming words, objects, and emotions, as you'll read about later.

ADD DRAMATIC DELIVERY

Content and concepts are equally important, and so is connecting the two. Teachers can convey information in ways that help learners absorb both content and concepts. I call this technique *dramatic delivery*. No matter their age, children and adults learn better when ideas are presented in a dramatic way. Using dramatic delivery doesn't mean you should always be overly emotional when you teach. There are many ways to share your passion for any subject. Being willing to find many ways to bring information to life is most important. Artistic integration is often the key for successful dramatic delivery. Whether role-playing characters from a book or using play-based approaches with songs, rhymes, and sign language, you can use dramatic delivery to encourage lifelong learning.

Aiming for True Growth

Today young children are often put into stressful situations that impact their childhood, their approach to life, and the many decisions they will make as young adults. Stressful situations come from many different sources, including parents, peers, and from within. There are thousands of ways stress and pressure can sneak into children's lives. As educators, we must do all we can to help our children protect themselves from the stress and pressure we sometimes equate with success and life. Before we can teach this lesson to children, we must learn to embrace it ourselves.

The Life Learning Techniques, which are both artistic and holistic, have helped adults improve how they guide children. Teaching is a great challenge and a great thrill. As a teacher (and parent), I ask myself regularly, "How do I want to use my energy?" This question has taken my interactions with children to a new level.

To quote my dear friend and mentor Dr. Carroll Rinehart, "For growth to take place, one must be willing to risk, and for risk to take place, there must be trust." Losing our tempers and being impatient or inflexible with children diminishes trust. If children do not trust their teachers, they will be less willing to take risks, which will lead to less growth. Some content-based growth can still occur without trust, but true growth of depth rarely takes place without trust.

By content-based growth, I mean the acquisition of knowledge. By growth of depth, I mean the ability to apply knowledge and use it in new ways, as opposed to only following directions. Structure and rules do and should exist, but children must be able to adapt rules and knowledge in order to venture into uncharted territory. Great people are individuals who have taken risks, such as Beethoven, Lincoln, Picasso, and Martin Luther King Jr. The next great scientist, the next world-class artist, the next pioneer in business is in your classroom. You can help these children trust enough to take risks and risk enough to truly grow.

Chapter 6

• • • • • • • • • • •

Add Music

Have you ever been in a restaurant with family and friends and noticed that the music in the background was just a bit too loud (or maybe *way* too loud)? Maybe the music had a fast tempo, in addition to being loud, and you found yourself eating faster, talking faster, and speaking louder as a result. Even if you don't recall a moment like this, you have likely responded to music in this very way. Welcome to the wonderful world of commerce in which companies use music to change consumer habits.

There is a beautiful grocery store in the city where I live. It is a high-end establishment, and its products are pricy, but it is a fun place to visit, especially if you're an amateur chef like me. Along with the relaxing and breathtaking visual stimuli of the store, early classical music by composers such as Bach, Handel, Vivaldi, Corelli, and Mozart often plays in the background, most of which has a tempo of about sixty beats per minute. Dr. Alfred Tomatis (Ostrander and Schroeder 1994) has shown that the frequencies produced by the main instruments of early classical compositions are the most conducive to healthy cognition. The audio and visual cues in this grocery store are telling my brain, more than anything else, "Take your time." The sixty-beats-per-minute music slows my pulse and inspires me to do something I often forget to do—take a deep breath.

The music in this grocery store impacts the environment, which in turn affects human behavior. More to the point, the grocery store's auditory environment encourages shoppers to stay a while, giving them more opportunities to purchase groceries. The music sets a particular mood for customers. Did the owners of the store choose early classical music by design? Did they know it would impact customer behavior? I'm not sure. I just know that I feel relaxed when I shop—there is no high-pressure selling going on—which means my brain has the chance to process information more completely and accurately.

Findings on Music's Physical Effects

According to psychiatrist Dr. Judith Carlson et al. (2004), brain function improves with relaxation and appropriate music. Their research shows, for example, that relaxation and music improve reading performance. Music and relaxation affect our mental performance, and our mental performance influences every aspect of our lives. Adding music to environments can be a simple and powerful way to improve lifestyle and learning.

The relationship between soothing music and a relaxed mental state is well established, and research confirms that relaxation affects the body's physiology in ways that lead to a more proficient brain:

- Dr. Georgi Lozanov played baroque music for his patients and found that body rhythms—heartbeat, brain waves, and blood pressure—slowed down and synchronized to the beat of the music (Ostrander and Schroeder 1979).

- Edward B. Blanchard conducted an experiment in which he played music for students during a classroom examination. Students in the experimental group had dramatically lower blood pressure and scored significantly higher on the exam than students in the control group, who did not have music playing in the background during the exam (Carlson et al. 2004).

• Anderson et al. (2000) showed that when music is used in learning situations, academic outcomes are improved, as well as students' general mind-set. The study also connects the use of background music to improved retention of spelling words.

These are just some of the studies that link music, environment, and relaxation with improved brain function and better academic performance.

Findings on Music's Emotional Effects

Research also confirms the calming effect of music; rhythm, in particular, appears to lead to relaxation. One of the first changes in our bodies when we are under stress is an increased pulse. Slow external rhythms (fifty to sixty beats per minute) can slow our pulse, resulting in a more relaxed physiological state (Carslon et al. 2004). In addition, there is relationship between music and mood, tension, and mental clarity. Research shows that music designed to promote mental and emotional balance can increase the beneficial effects of positive emotional states on the immune system (McCraty et al. 1998). This organization's principles have been widely adopted by Fortune 500 companies, hospitals, clinics, and schools.

Adding music to the environment can have some ultrapositive effects, but it can also have negative effects when misused. I can give a high-end bar and restaurant in my town as an example. Before I enter this particular restaurant itself, I walk through its plush, beautifully designed bar. The bar is upbeat and positive but not calm, and it is full of people. A live jazz trio plays great swing tunes in the background, and then fast bebop selections, and then upbeat Latin jazz tunes. The group doesn't play ballads or anything slow. I know the musicians who play at this restaurant, and I confirmed that they never play anything with a tempo under eighty beats per minute. Why? The restaurant's policy is to play only upbeat music.

This policy sounds innocent, but the upbeat music is meant to attract people to the establishment and keep their energy and heart rates up so they drink faster, eat faster, spend more money, and quickly open up seats for more patrons. It doesn't end at the bar. When I enter the restaurant, I almost skip to my chair, because it's difficult to saunter to big band music. There's nothing wrong with big band music—I love it and I've performed it many times—but the restaurant only plays the upbeat songs from that era, no beautiful ballads. I don't mind some upbeat music while I'm eating. I just don't like hearing it constantly when I'm trying to enjoy my dinner, taste my red wine, and speak to my wife in a normal tone of voice. I haven't been back to that restaurant in more than five years.

Some business owners worry so much about receiving a certain dollar amount per patron, they fail to see the value of repeat business. I like to be able to chew my food slowly, taste it, sink into a calm state, and enjoy the entire dining experience. In addition to that, I know my body absorbs nutrients better if my heart rate is slower and I am relaxed. According to Nora Gedgaudas (2009), a certified nutritional therapist (CNT) and a board-certified clinical neurofeedback specialist (CNS) with twenty-five years of experience in holistic nutrition, chewing your protein foods well and eating in a relaxed environment improve how your body digests and uses food.

Luckily, more and more businesses are treating their auditory environments with care. Many normal grocery stores—not just high-end—now play relaxing music to help customers feel good, which makes customers want to return. It's good for business, and it's good for you. If you pay attention, you'll find many examples of music influencing the environments in your life. Most people just let music affect them unconsciously, and while there is nothing wrong with that, we can become more conscious of how music is used in our environments on a daily basis—at our homes and in our schools.

Dancing with the Corti Chorus Line

Music influences environments in many ways based on its type, tempo, pitch, and general intent, but it impacts more than just the environment. I use high-frequency music, for example, in professional development with teachers and in working with young children. Violin, piano, flute, guitar, and voice produce the richest high frequencies, and all of these instruments are present in early classical and baroque music. In his work, Dr. Alfred Tomatis explores the relationship between these frequencies and the human ear. As Sheila Ostrander and Lynne Schroeder (1994, 111) noted when reflecting on Tomatis's work, "Something outside of you charges up your battery cells and that something is *sound*, particularly high-frequency sound."

The *cochlea* is the auditory processing portion of the inner ear. The core component of the cochlea is the *organ of Corti*, also referred to as the *Corti cells*. The Corti cells are the remarkable middlemen of our inner ear. As Ostrander and Schroeder (1994, 111–12) describe:

> If you took a trip through your inner ear, after whirling around and around through the labyrinthine swirls of the snail-shaped cochlea, you'd suddenly come upon the "Corti chorus line." Arranged in rows, these 24,600 long-stemmed cells move with perfect precision to each sound. . . . The energy produced by this extraordinary dance flows to your brain, and some of it also splits off through the vestibular branch of your auditory nerve and flashes to the muscles of your body. High-frequency sound energizes your brain while at the same time, it releases muscle tension and balances the body in many other ways. It even affects your posture."

According to Tomatis (Ostrander and Schroeder 1994), sound, resonance, and rhythm greatly affect learning, health, and productivity. Beneficial high-frequency sounds exist in early classical and baroque music. This kind of music, which includes Bach's sonatas and Mozart's concertos, has inherent patterns and sequences that can help shape young children's brain development.

Sound, in the form of music in this case, travels in waves that humans perceive as pitch. Each pitch, or musical note, corresponds to a particular frequency that can be measured in hertz (Hz). Recent scientific breakthroughs make it possible to identify the benefits of specific musical keys and resonances. For example, Ostrander and Schroeder (1994, 109–10) report that "the key of G (194.71 Hz) resonates with the color orange-red, and has a dynamic, stimulating, and energizing effect on the body-mind. The key of C-sharp (136.10 Hz) resonates with the color turquoise-green. This is a calming, meditative, relaxing, and centering key. The key of F (172.06 Hz) resonates with the color purple-violet. It has a joyful, cheerful, and spiritual effect."

Linking Environment, Action, and Emotion

A critical factor in human behavior is emotion, including how we grow emotionally, how we learn to harness our emotions, and how we use the energy of emotion wisely. Music can impact emotion just as much as it impacts environments and behaviors (Davies, Roberts, and Slankov 1998). Researchers at McGill University (Salimpoor et al. 2011), for example, found that that music activates both the cognitive and limbic systems of the brain; the limbic system is the part of the brain connected to emotion. These researchers also found that listening to music triggers a release of dopamine, a chemical associated with the experience of reward.

It is breathtaking to hear, feel, and sense the change in a learning environment when music is used to guide learning. Using music in combination with relaxation, breathing, and focused play-based games also leads to better health. Terminology—such as *imaginative rehearsal, visualization,* and *the mind's eye*—and our understanding of them change over time. Use whichever term floats your boat. Successful people—and I define *success* broadly—have strong minds and are able to stay focused on the positive aspects of life. Happy children are more likely to be successful, and music can help us create joyful and uplifting environments. We can create high-frequency, calming, and empowering auditory environments in our cars, outside, in our homes, at work, in our classrooms, and everywhere we go.

Practice
Moments for Music

In general, you can use music in two major ways:

- indirectly to affect learning environments or heart rates

- directly as part of an activity or in the study and performance of music

There are many ways to use music to improve learning environments and learning. Below are four essential ways—two for indirect use and two for direct use—you can use music in your early childhood classroom to improve children's learning and behavior.

1. Changing Learning Environments (usually an indirect use)

Certain kinds of music can change the mood of any room. Changing the mood of a classroom with music can make certain kinds of learning easier and certain interactions more likely. For example, upbeat classical music—with a tempo of 120 beats per minute—could inspire a quiet child to open up and begin to interact.

In what learning areas in your classroom could you include music? When and how would you use music? List a few of your ideas here.

_____

_____

_____

_____

2. Changing Mind-Body States of Being (indirect or direct use)

Using music to change mind-body states of being is a lot like using it to change environments. In fact, both can happen simultaneously. The effect of music on mind-body states is well known. Some hospitals, for example, recommend thirty to forty minutes of slow baroque or classical music to help calm patients.

In your classroom, use slow classical music with a tempo of about sixty beats per minute to calm children, help them focus, help relieve their fears, improve their memory, and so on. Nonclassical music at the same tempo —including slow jazz and environmental music, such as sounds of the forest, ocean, and rainfall—can have the same effect.

How might you use music in your classroom to calm children? In what learning areas would calming music be helpful? During which activities? List a few of your ideas here.

_____

_____

_____

_____

3. Using Music with Activities (direct use)

By using music with activities, you are taking a powerful step toward teaching to all learning styles and making learning easier for all children. For example, by using music in the Surfing the Words game (page 146), you address children who are visual learners (looking at the book), auditory learners (hearing music and words), and kinesthetic learners (acting out what is going on in the book). You could add music while the children are fingerpainting. Fingerpainting is already a highly visual and kinesthetic activity. The introduction of music adds auditory learning to the activity, awakens specific brain centers, and helps children balance organized structure and creativity.

In what classroom activities could you introduce music? What new music-related activities could you introduce to the children? List a few of your ideas here.

_____

_____

_____

_____

4. Using Music during Transition Times (direct use)

Master teachers do not teach discipline. Instead, they engage children at such a high level that discipline is a natural result. Transition times can be challenging and a test to children's behavior because teachers often do not use these times for learning and having fun. To ease a transition, you could use music in a game-based way. When children come inside from the outdoors, for example, you could make breathing sounds that imitate the sound of a train. Not only is this game fun for children, but it will calm them down if done correctly. To take the game further, instead of saying, "Line up so we can go inside," you could say, "Choo choo time!" This could be a cue for children to make a "train" by lining up and to make train sounds with breathing techniques. As another option, you could add slow classical music to the background to ease transition time; doing so would also help auditory learners engage.

Think of the transition times in your day with children, such as when children have to wash their hands, brush their teeth, or clean up. How might you incorporate music to improve these transition times? List a few of your ideas here.

_____

_____

_____

_____

You can use various styles of music with each approach. I often use European classical music, but I also use music from many other cultures and periods. Whatever style you use, find music that has short, long, and extended patterns and music that has an emotional punch. In other words, find music that has depth and quality. Remember, choose the music carefully; specific kinds of music affect performance, mood, and more in specific ways. The table below shows my suggested balance of music for the early childhood classroom.

Baroque/classical	50%
Jazz	15%
Multicultural/world	30%
Selected pop/rock	5%

Exactly what music should you use? Which composers? Which movements? Which arrangements? To start, see the sample music lists in the appendix (page 173) for selections I have found useful in my work at the Fostering Arts-Mind Education Foundation. This list is just a starting point. I encourage you to keep exploring and to add your own music to the list. I encourage you to keep looking for new ways to use music in your classroom.

Chapter 7
. . . .

Affirm

Affirmations are statements that we say or think about others or ourselves. They are comments about who we think we are and who we think others are. The most powerful affirmations are those we say to ourselves—*self-affirmations.* Self-affirmations, whether positive or negative, impact our attitudes, decisions, and self-concept. Positive affirmations are the brother of confidence. Negative affirmations nurture pessimism and self-loathing. Many people think of an affirmation as simply a pat on the back, but we must look deeper. Affirmation is an umbrella under which all learning takes place for young children.

Developing a Positive Self-Concept Early

We all have moments in our lives when we ask ourselves questions about what we can accomplish or what we have accomplished. These moments are a part of growing up, and they shape and refine our self-concept. As young people transition from childhood to adolescence, they begin to question what they can or can't achieve. For many, this test of self-confidence starts in late elementary school or in middle school. For others, questioning starts in high school. For children living in stressful situations, questioning can begin very early in life and can become an ongoing challenge.

While there are several critical junctures for social-emotional development, children's first big step in developing a sense of self occurs when they are very young, from prebirth through age five or six. In an article for the National Association for the Education of Young Children (NAEYC), University of Florida child researchers Kristen Kemple and Stacy Ellis (2009, 5) write that "a full description of social competence involves a broad range of values, knowledge, and concepts about self and others." They go on to state that social competence develops in early childhood. They define social competence as having a "positive self-identity; interpersonal skills, self-regulation, planning, and decision-making skills; cultural competence; and social values" (Kemple and Ellis 2009, 5). Affirmation is closely linked to all of these areas of social growth, especially to positive self-identity. One of the most critical times for adults to be positive, uplifting forces for children, then, is when children are very young.

Teaching Test-Taking Skills versus Critical-Thinking Skills

Helping children develop a positive self-concept with ongoing affirmation should be easy and should be a part of every child's experience in education, but we live in a unique society that defines education in a narrow manner. Many leading educators believe that many of the challenges in education lie in education policy, teacher development, and parent education. Teachers need more support. These comments are not a reflection on teachers but, rather, the policies that can sometimes dictate our choices if we aren't careful.

Our education policy tends to focus on teaching test-taking skills rather than critical-thinking skills. I visit and work in many schools throughout the country—including preschools and elementary, middle, and high schools—and have found that concept is often over-shadowed by content. Concept and content should be connected, and they can be connected if schools take time to carefully and thoughtfully develop a vision, curriculum, and delivery system. Knowing content in any area of study is important, of course, but if we don't help children develop deeper understandings of concepts, their knowledge will become useless after they have taken a test and have moved on to another topic.

Students must be engaged in learning for critical thinking to occur. As teachers, we can find ways to engage students so they become lifelong learners who are hungry to learn and eager to explore. To start, we can develop a setting of trust where students see teachers as guides offering opportunities for growth. An environment of trust fosters bold and discovery-based attitudes toward learning. It fosters children who see learning as a process. Conversely, an environment without trust—where teachers control and dominate thinking—creates children who are afraid to take risks. These children begin to rely on direction from others, and this reliance can damage their self-concept. This damage can be reversed, but it takes time and requires uplifting people in an environment of trust.

Realizing the Power of Our Inner Thoughts

Affirmation is one of the ingredients for developing a strong self-concept. A strong self-concept leads to social competence, and social and emotional intelligence are key elements for success. Do you know anyone who has a difficult time receiving compliments? This common behavior is a sign of a developing self-concept. True lifelong learners realize, of course, that development is an ongoing process. It is all about evolving.

Self-talk, also called *inner thoughts*, drives our understanding of who we are and what we can achieve. Our inner thoughts are connected to both our conscious and subconscious minds. When we are awake and alert, our conscious mind makes decisions and distinguishes between fact and fiction. When we sleep, our conscious mind takes a break and our subconscious mind works in its place.

The road between the conscious and subconscious minds goes two ways; our conscious self-talk affects our subconscious self-talk and vice versa. We need to pay attention to our inner thoughts and keep them positive; both our conscious and subconscious minds will benefit. The famous saying by Napoleon Hill, "What the mind of man can conceive and believe, it can achieve," carries a lot of truth.

Affirmations can significantly impact our lives and the lives of children. When children hear harsh words, see negative body language, or hear nice words with a sarcastic tone, their self-concept is being affected negatively. Children's conscious and subconscious minds are taking in the information. When we repeatedly receive negative emotions from others, we become confused and lose confidence over time. Self-concept is fragile and can be damaged. Imagine how easily the self-concept of a three-year-old could be damaged.

With a strong self-concept, we invent, launch business ventures, and take on artistic endeavors to explore our mind and soul. With a battered self-concept, we focus on what we lack, what others have taken, and how to survive; this is not living fully, and it is not living like a child. Living like a child means living with an exuberance that borders on giddiness. It means living with focus, confidence, and calmness and enjoying every moment. Our thoughts drive our actions and our energy, and they have a power we can either ignore or engage.

Affirming through Love Languages

In his book *The Five Love Languages: How to Express Heartfelt Commitment to Your Mate*, Dr. Gary Chapman (1992) describes the five love languages people use to express and receive love:

1. physical touch

2. words of affirmation

3. quality time

4. acts of service

5. gifting

We all prefer one or several of these love languages over the others, and we usually have at least one language we prefer the least. We also may prefer one language for receiving love and another for giving love. Love languages are like learning styles in that people benefit when they become versatile and learn multiple ways of loving. We should embrace our strengths but work to improve our weaknesses. Teachers can easily identify children's love languages by observing their behaviors.

Knowing how you and the children prefer to express love is an important step to improving children's self-concept. When you are able to speak a child's love language, you have a much better chance of connecting with that child. Trust is established at a very high level when someone knows he or she is loved. The affirmations you use are meaningful.

PHYSICAL TOUCH

A person who prefers to express love with physical touch is sometimes called a hugger. A child who hugs you often, asks for a kiss, or likes to rub your arm or your shirt speaks the love language of physical touch.

WORDS OF AFFIRMATION

A person who prefers words of affirmation is a person who thrives on praise, specifically words of praise, such as "Great job!" or "Do you know how fantastic you are?" or "I'm so proud of you!" These people not only prefer to receive their love in words, but they best understand that they are loved when told so in words.

QUALITY TIME

I call children who need quality time *QT kids*. If you ask a QT kid, "How do you know I love you?" the child might respond with, "You hang out with me" or "You listen to what I have to say." For children who prefer this love language, *being* with them is most important. The quality time can occur anywhere at any time—for example, over a meal or while shopping at a grocery store—as long as you are completely engaged in the interaction.

ACTS OF SERVICE

This is the love language that my amazing and beautiful wife prefers to receive! If I want to put a huge smile on her face, I just have to do something for her. It doesn't have to be anything earth shattering; the act of service is often as simple as washing the dishes, pulling weeds in the yard, or getting her a glass of water. Doing the act of service without being asked is the key to connecting with speakers of this love language.

GIFTING

The fifth love language is expressed by giving gifts. The gift doesn't have to be expensive. The act of giving itself is what matters. People who speak the love language of gifting light up the moment they give a gift.

Watch how children interact with others so you can speak to them in their love language. Who are your how-about-a-hug kids? Your pat-on-the-back kids? Your let's-hang-out-together kids? Your do-something-for-me kids? Your here's-my-gift kid? If a child hugs you, it is really important to hug him back. If a child beams when you give her words of praise, remember that's how she likes to be energized! Notice which children like to be around you a lot, and give them the simple gift of quality time together. Notice which children wait to be helped by you and then beam when you do help. These children are wired to receive love through acts of service. Watch for the child who brings you a pebble, some dirt, a flower, a Lego, a penny, or the lint from inside his pocket. Don't brush off these gifts; this child is taking a risk by reaching out to you. Try responding to this child in different ways until you see a connection through his eyes.

Letting children know you love them in both your love language and theirs is critical. It is a simple thing to do, but it forces you to be completely open. Saying "I love you" is not enough if your body language says something else. I have seen the important role of love in my work with children. I have also seen some of the finest early childhood educators, such as dramatic-play guru and author Mimi Chenfeld and music-education leader Dr. Carroll Rinehart, use their knowledge of love when working with children. Children who know they are loved learn how to love others and want to express love themselves. Someone who takes the risk of expressing love develops an immensely strong self-concept, which leads to self-confidence and trust and, ultimately, growth.

Affirming through Play

Take advantage of everyday opportunities to let children know you value them, respect them, and love them, while still being their guide. Sometimes opportunities are not obvious to adults but are very natural for children. To connect with young children, for example, you must play games; that is, you must turn learning situations into games and find ways to teach through play. Lectures and talking are not ways to engage a young child's interest. Conjure up the Master Teaching Principle of improvisation when you affirm through play.

In the same way the commercial world creates one-line descriptions of product lines, we must be simple in our affirmations. Simple does not mean dumbing down or underestimating a child's ability to infer and understand. We can build children's vocabulary and expose them to many advanced concepts while offering simple affirmations to keep them exploring on their own. By offering affirmations—especially in ways that involve play and children's interests—you increase the possibility that children's potential will be realized. You are letting children know they matter and that they can achieve anything.

Affirming through Positive Language

The affirmations you give to children are more than just statements of how amazing you think they are. When you affirm children with language, try to use words that have strong positive connotations. For example, I use the word *champion* more often than *winner.* I use *winner* in context, but I use the word *champion* more frequently because it has greater depth. *Winner* implies that there is a loser. *Champion* means someone is being the best she or he can be. Some people might think the word *winner* is more appropriate, claiming that the "real world" works in terms of winners and losers. In life, of course, we all experience situations where we win or we lose, but ponder the following questions:

- Do we want children to define themselves as winners or losers based on whether they win or lose at a certain event in life?

- Do we think children will not have enough opportunities to win or lose in their lives?

Our children will have many opportunities to compete in their lives. Instead of defining winners and losers, let's make sure our children have the inner fortitude to get back up when they don't win—because that's what champions do. Building children's self-concept and affirming them isn't about winning and losing. It's about seeing children as individuals who can achieve in the short-term and long-term, even when obstacles arise.

Realizing the Power of Affirmation

Harnessing the power of affirmation cannot be outlined in a simple step-by-step formula because there are many things you can say and do to help children focus on the positive. When I was in eighth grade, for example, my mom helped me write my four-year goals. My goals were all related to music and education. I remember the list—written in red ink with jagged handwriting on a piece of crumply paper—only because my mom whipped it out when I graduated from high school. In her infinite wisdom, she had kept this piece of paper. We sat down at the breakfast table, and she handed it to me with pride shining in her eyes. I looked at the paper with astonishment and read the goals. Then I smiled. I accomplished all of the goals. Did I accomplish these goals magically? Of course not. I put forth a great deal of effort in those interim years. And the effort was initiated by powerful, meaningful self-affirmations that came from within me.

Teachers can only watch children grow, even though we might want to grow for them. We want children to succeed without strife, without pain, and without self-doubt, but allowing them to do so would be folly. The joys of life are sometimes made sweeter because of negative or challenging experiences. Children will make mistakes, but with affirmations, they can learn from their mistakes. By offering affirmations, we can help children develop a strong self-concept. In the end, that self-concept—how children see themselves—will contain the one opinion that matters most in their lives.

Practice

Kiss Your Brain

This play-based activity works wonders for many children. The technique even works with adults and has been known to put smiles on the faces of even the most serious grown-ups.

Key

Primary learning style: kinesthetic
Domain: social-emotional development
Specific academic area: literacy (positional words and vocabulary expansion)
Educational bonus: self-confidence
Suggested music: slow or fast early classical music (60 or 120 beats per minute, depending on accompanying games)
Materials needed: music source and enthusiasm

Demonstrate the actions as you say to the children, "Take your hand and kiss it. Now, take your hand—Be careful! There's a freshly planted kiss on it!—and put it on your head. That's where your brain is . . . I hope!"

If you like to multitask, you can turn the affirmation-focused Kiss Your Brain game into a literacy game by saying the following as you play:

- Kiss the side of your brain.

- Kiss the top of your brain.

- Kiss the back of your brain.

- Kiss the front of your brain.

- Kiss above your brain.

- Kiss behind your brain.

- Kiss to the left of your brain.

- Kiss to the right of your brain.

Kiss Your Brain is a perfect game to help you transition to another activity. I use this game whenever I see a moment to affirm the children.

Variation

Once, after I asked children to kiss their brains, a young child asked me, "Can we kiss our hearts?" I thought, "Wow, the love and care that young children show is amazing!" So, if you'd like, you can also incorporate this idea.

Practice

Give Yourself a Hug

Another play-based way to affirm young children— and to get them stretching to increase flexibility—is to ask them to give themselves a hug. Some children may not want to hug themselves, but most children will love the idea.

Key

Primary learning style: kinesthetic
Domain: social-emotional development
Specific academic area: literacy (comprehension)
Educational bonus: self-confidence
Suggested music: slow early classical music (sixty beats per minute)
Materials needed: a smile and generosity

Think of this game as a transition activity and an organic way to build self-love and confidence. I use it often and at many times during the day to help children move from one activity to another. For example, I sometimes ask children to hug themselves when they come back inside from the outdoors. You can do this activity almost anywhere. Improvise!

When a children or adults hug themselves, they cross their midlines. When we cross the middle of our bodies with our hands, arms, or legs, we help synchronize the left and right sides of our brain. This helps children improve many areas of performance, including the early literacy skill of tracking words with their eyes across the middle of any book. Another excellent variation to Give Yourself a Hug is asking the children to switch the placement of their arms, either left over right or right over left. This aids in cognitive growth related, again, to the crossing of the midline.

Once, a child who did not want to hug himself did feel like becoming a tree. So I invited him to do so, and I became a tree as well. I then asked if he wanted to give himself a "tree hug" and he said with an enormous smile, "Yes!" The point is, be ready and willing to incorporate children's tangents and original ideas into your plans because this is when magic can occur. Children take ownership through their ideas, and by using their ideas, you can keep children engaged. In this way, you can encourage the development of inventive minds and minimize the development of minds that simply consume and follow directions.

Chapter 8

· · · · · · · · · · ·

Breathe and Relax

When I talk about breathing and relaxing, I don't mean everyday breathing and I don't mean relaxing at the beach. I'm talking about breathing and relaxation techniques that are thousands of years old and included in yoga, qigong, and Zen practices.

- Breathing is a basic component of the yoga technique called *pranayama*. The word *pranayama* can be broken down into two Sanskrit words, *prana* meaning life force and *ayama* meaning control. Thus, *pranayama* means controlling (or using) the flow of life force. This practice dates back approximately thirty-five hundred years.

- *Qigong* exists in many forms or schools. *Qigong* originated in China and dates back approximately two thousand years.

- Zen breathing also dates back thousands of years. Zen as a specific form was first documented in 700 CE. Within Zen practice is *anapanasati*. The word can be broken into *sati*, meaning mindfulness, and *anapana*, meaning to inhale and exhale. *Anapanasati*, then, means mindful breathing.

These techniques share a common trait: they acknowledge breathing as a key component in training the mind and strengthening energy.

I use breathing and relaxation techniques as a professional musician, but I find these techniques even more important in my personal life; I use breathing exercises to improve my ability to be relaxed and focused every day. With relaxed focus, I can enjoy the simple pleasures of many moments.

Breathing and Visualization

Olympic athletes use breathing techniques with visualization to prepare for competition. Visualization— addressed in chapter 9—and breathing go hand in hand because skillful visualization requires relaxation and focus. For example, during a match and in practice, tennis great Roger Federer breathes deeply and visualizes the exact trajectory of the ball and the angle of his stroke. He does not take shallow breaths through his chest like most people. He takes deep breaths that involve the abdomen. Doing so helps him become physically relaxed and mentally alert simultaneously.

Athletes have been using breathing and visualization techniques to improve performance and to get into "the zone" for a long time, but these breathing techniques can be used by anyone. When you simultaneously become physically relaxed and mentally alert in your everyday life, you can achieve more, enjoy experiences more, and lead others more effectively. When you achieve this state of being as your daily way of living, marvelous things can and do happen. You will change not only the way you live, but the energy you radiate. This energy is a key to becoming truly successful. A relaxed body, attained through breathing and movement techniques, leads to an alert and highly functioning mind, which improves performance in many areas.

The last time I searched online for "breathing, relaxation, and visualization" on the Internet, I came up with 270,000 links. In my work with children and teachers, and in my own life, I've developed techniques that build on some of the well-known breathing techniques used throughout the ages.

Breathing in Music Training and Beyond

I found joy in playing and listening to music at a young age. My mom used to sing and play recordings of music for me. I remember hearing Mexican and Spanish folk songs and Beethoven's symphonies. I grew up singing in church choirs, playing the piano, and taking tuba lessons. My development in music as a child was a lot like the development of food preferences. With food, we develop a taste for simple foods first and then come to appreciate more complex tastes and textures over time.

Musicians, especially singers and wind instrument players, learn many breathing techniques as they grow. They learn to breathe deeply and control airflow in order to sing or play their instrument skillfully. My instructors, for example, taught me how to breathe in a focused and intense way while remaining relaxed. Even though the breathing techniques alone were not music, I learned that the techniques were one of the components that made music possible.

Breathing is a simple technique, but it can have healing and empowering effects in music. When I was on the faculty at the University of Wisconsin, I had the great pleasure of working with the legendary choral conductor Robert Fountain and singing in his choir. Robert Fountain connected with many people through music. Did we breathe deeply during his choral rehearsals? Most certainly. Using breathing techniques while creating music or art is one of the best ways to practice breathing properly for increased energy, improved focus, and improved overall health.

As a young musician, I thought I needed to relax and focus only to connect to the arts. I've found, however, that deep breathing and rhythmic breathing, married with a strong self-image and positive approach, has greatly affected my success in all areas. Not only has it made a difference in my professional life, but more importantly, it has increased the joy I am able to find in the everyday moments of life. To sustain a relaxed body and alert mind, we need energy, the ability to circulate energy, a strong mental approach focused on what is possible, and enough humility to know that we always have more to learn, refine, and adjust.

Breathing with Emotion

Breathing and relaxing are not separate things; I think of them as a single concept. Breathing deeply and relaxing physically occur at the same time and can result in mental focus. We don't often equate breathing and relaxation with mental focus. Instead, we imagine someone who is extremely relaxed as either sleeping or about to fall asleep, and we image someone with mental focus—for example, someone preparing for an important life event with focus—as having some level of stress. Most people I know are either relaxed or focused, but not both. It is possible, however, to live with intensity (focus) and also softness (relaxation). It is possible to balance life while being completely committed to each activity.

In other words, life is full of emotion, but emotion doesn't need to be at odds with calmness. Learning to breathe without emotion is healthy and can garner results, but learning to breathe while emotionally connecting gives us the energy needed to perform at the highest levels of life. The greatest professionals in any field—whether a musician at the height of a performance, a business owner presenting a marketing plan, or a teacher engaging a class of children—embrace the energy of the moment, while remaining focused and relaxed. The energy of the moment is sometimes referred to as being passionate for what you do. According to several of my colleagues, passion is why I was hired by the University of Arizona at the green age of twenty-five. Passion is often the reason we choose to follow particular leaders. When you can couple passion with a clear mind, you become a leader worthy of praise.

Reasons for Practicing Rhythmic Breathing

Why is *rhythmic breathing* (for example, breathing in for two seconds and out for four seconds) important? To answer this question, let's examine the definition of *rhythmic pollution*, a term I first heard from Janalea Hoffman, a pioneer in the field of music therapy and founder of Rhythmic Medicine. Think back to a day when farmers made up a larger part of our population. Farmers woke to the sound of a rooster or the glimmer of the sun. They ate a big breakfast and then worked throughout the day. They drank water when they were thirsty. Soda, oversized mineral- and sugar-infused sports drinks, and artificially flavored substances did not exist. The work of a farming family was rhythmic in nature—milking the cows, raking leaves, tilling the soil. The family ate dinner when the sun went down and often went to sleep soon after that. In the nineteenth century, and even the first half of the twentieth century, people's minds had opportunities to stop and rest. A home may have contained a radio or a television (one television for the entire household), but the sounds of loud commercials were not layered against sounds of a video game in a nearby room and of a handheld electronic game in another.

All sounds have vibrations. Today we are bombarded with vibrations, sounds, visual images, sound effects, low-end spectrum vibrations, and more on most days of our lives. With all of this rhythmic pollution, finding our own internal body rhythm is almost impossible. Rhythmic breathing can help us reconnect with that rhythm.

If you fill your classroom with layers of vibrations and sounds from the commercial world, rhythmic breathing may not help you or the children much. When you combine a healthy classroom environment with rhythmic breathing, however, you can create an environment that moves at a slower pace, which will allow you and the children to be more productive. Remember, a slower heart rate makes a quicker and more agile brain! Don't let someone else dictate the auditory environment of your classroom. Take control of it with a healthy selection of appropriate music.

Practicing Your Breathing

There are many ways to work on your breathing, but the best ways involve context, such as an art activity (music, dance, visual art, and drama) or sports. The arts, in particular, are unique because they engage children and adults physically, mentally, and emotionally, all with a sense of calm and power when practicing and performing. In addition, the arts are ultimately about continuing to find our best possible selves. In the arts, your greatest opponent is yourself.

Overall health is, of course, another critical component to successful breathing and vice versa. What we eat, what we drink, and how we exercise are all key components to a successful and joyful approach to life. Sing with children or have them play a wind instrument (brass or woodwind). Dance with them. Involve them in a sport where they move. Find activities that force you and the children to expand your breathing while being active.

Find time throughout your day to breathe deeply and rhythmically yourself so you can model relaxation and focus for children; you can use the adult breathing techniques at the end of this chapter to get started. If you feel you do not have enough time in your hectic day to add rhythmic breathing as a separate activity, integrate the breathing exercises into your established routine, such as when you are taking a shower, lying in bed, or sitting on a sofa.

Teaching Breathing to Children

The breathing and relaxation games for children (pages 103–14) will help you introduce slow, deep, and smooth breathing to young children in a play-based manner. Of course, you can and should teach breathing and other topics simultaneously. These games will also help you promote the *rhythmic delivery* of learning. Rhythmic delivery means delivering learning in a rhythmic and paced manner, rather than cramming it in. Rhythmic delivery implies repetition but not for repetition's sake. Rather, repetition is used to build on children's learning, allowing children time to absorb the basics while exploring other topics further. Using rhythmic delivery is important because it can give children—and adults—a lifelong method of learning and living. By understanding the basics of rhythmic delivery, we can become driven and successful but not consumed by drive and success. As guides, we can teach children the same skills. Learning with rhythmic delivery is learning with joy and a sense of discovery. I continue to teach myself to live this way every day.

In a nutshell, rhythmic delivery involves the following:

- having a relaxed body and alert mind

- breathing with slow sixty-beats-per-minute music

- hearing and becoming content and concepts with visual stimuli

- hearing and becoming content and concepts without visual stimuli

Research shows that improved learning and memory take place over time when children are physically relaxed and mentally alert; when they breathe rhythmically (with or without music); when they can see (visual learning), hear (auditory learning), and become (kinesthetic learning) content and concepts; and when they visualize what they are seeing and hearing. Rhythmic delivery, then, will help children absorb and remember what they learn. I've found rhythmic delivery to be particularly effective after energetic play.

Find many play-based ways to integrate rhythmic delivery, breathing, and relaxation in your work with young children. Help them to explore and continue to love learning for what it truly is, an ongoing exploration of life.

Practice

Entering the Performance Zone

Your goal with this breathing practice is to relax your physical body while keeping your mind alert; this is the optimal state of mind and body for performance

in any situation, including situations that involve making decisions, dealing with stress, studying, playing sports, making music, and leading. Try to practice this exercise at least three times a day: morning, afternoon, and evening. As with any kind of exercise, consult your doctor before using these exercises, especially if you are on any kind of medication.

Step 1: Deep Breathing and Movement

This first step will elevate your heart rate and your energy level. The use of slow, sixty-beats-per-minute classical music is recommended for steps 1 and 2.

1. Begin by inhaling through your nose and exhaling through your mouth.

2. Breathe slowly, smoothly, and deeply (do not pause at the top of the breath).

3. Imagine a balloon inside your stomach and chest area and let it expand evenly on all sides as you inhale and exhale.

4. Focus your thoughts on something relaxing, calming, or empowering.

5. Repeat steps 1 through 5 until you feel an improved sense of relaxation (at least a minute).

6. Add stretching as you continue to breathe.

7. Inhale as you start the stretch. Then hold your breath (without tensing up) and hold the stretch for approximately ten seconds. Exhale as you release the stretch.

8. Over time, work toward holding the stretch for up to thirty seconds.

   Note: Holding your breath while stretching (without tensing up) will help energize you. If you need to calm down and lower your heart rate, breathe through the stretches.

Usually stretches recommended by your doctor or personal trainer are appropriate, but physical therapists often have the best information on stretching. When you stretch, hold each stretch for approximately ten seconds and do several repetitions. Do not bounce the stretch; bouncing is a small trauma for those muscles. Stretching should not be the first step before any type of physical activity. Warm up your muscles with movement first, and then stretch. Use stretches that focus on areas of your body that are sore or stiff. Try to incorporate stretching into your daily routine.

After you have practiced a smooth and relaxed routine of deep breathing and stretching for a couple weeks, measure your heart rate. Count your pulse for ten seconds and then multiply that number by six to obtain your beats per minute. Record your heart rate. Your heart rate should be slightly or moderately elevated, depending on your physical condition. Give yourself time to become accustomed to these exercises. Some bodies and minds need more practice than others, but these techniques can be learned by everyone.

Step 2: Rhythmic Breathing

This second step will lower your heart rate, keep your energy level up, and increase your mental focus.

1. Use the second hand on a watch or clock to help you regulate your breathing. Inhale through your nose for two seconds and exhale through your mouth for four seconds.

2. Repeat this at least eight times.

3. Next, inhale for three seconds and exhale for six seconds.

4. Repeat this four to six times. **Note:** If the three-six breathing feels awkward, don't go on to the four-eight pattern. Work on the three-six pattern until it feels comfortable before moving on.

5. Now, inhale for four seconds and exhale for eight seconds. Remember to inhale through your nose and exhale through your mouth.

6. Repeat the four-eight pattern two or three times. After you have become comfortable with this slow, deep breathing, add more repetitions.

7. Go back to the three-six pattern and repeat it two to four times.

8. Go back to the two-four pattern and repeat it at least eight times.

   Note: Inhale smoothly, completing your breath by the last count. If you are on the four-eight pattern, try to be halfway full of breath at two seconds. When you exhale, gradually release all of your air so that you are out of air on the last count; try to be halfway out of breath at four seconds.

After you have completed this breathing exercise, measure your heart rate again and write it down. Ideally, your heart rate will be at about sixty beats per minute. Rates will vary based on metabolic rate. A number of things can affect your heart rate, including medications, being overweight, or experiencing stress.

Step 3: Adding Music

Adding music while you breathe in a focused, rhythmic manner can be very helpful in reducing stress. Slow classical music at approximately sixty beats per minute is the most helpful.

- You can use early classical music performed live with real instruments, but be aware that the tempo may fluctuate. This fluctuation can be a good thing because it makes you listen more carefully to the music.

- You can also use electronically created music in a classical style. The tempo will be very steady and will not fluctuate. This makes breathing rhythmically a little easier. The one drawback is that electronically created music may not have the same energy as live music.

Practice

Muscle Relaxation

This practice is a varia-
tion of Entering the Per-
formance Zone and is
designed to help you relax
your muscles.

Key

Primary learning style: kinesthetic

Domain: social-emotional development

Specific academic areas: applies to all

Educational bonus: ability to focus and improved
circulation

Suggested music: slow classical music (sixty beats
per minute)

Materials needed: music source (optional)

1. Think of something
   that makes you feel very peaceful. Play very soft and peaceful
   music in the background if it helps.

2. Imagine your body and your muscles being relaxed and
   heavy.

3. Without visual or auditory distractions, take a slow, deep,
   and smooth breath.

4. As you exhale, imagine your body floating and feel the
   emotion of gratefulness.

5. Repeat steps 3 and 4 until you feel an increased sense of
   peace.

6. Continue the cycle of breathing but begin to hold your
   breath for short periods without tensing up. As you hold
   your breath, stretch a muscle or targeted group of muscles
   for approximately five seconds.

7. Choose a muscle or group of muscles that have been feeling
   tight. Repeat this at least three times.

8. Repeat step 7, focusing on another group of muscles.

9. End your session with slow breathing that becomes increasingly deeper.

To bring this exercise to a close, awaken your body. This can be done in many ways. You can use certain herbal scents, such as peppermint or cinnamon. You can use laughter by watching a funny movie or playing a game that makes you laugh. Find the way that works best for you.

Practice

Expanding Breathing Capability

Most people breathe in a shallow manner. This exercise will help you sustain a long, smooth, and deep breath. Deep breathing is important in all of the breathing exercises presented in this section.

Key

Primary learning style: kinesthetic
Domain: physical development
Specific academic areas: applies to all
Educational bonus: self-regulation and the ability to focus
Suggested music: none
Materials needed: healthy lungs

1. Start a slow, smooth, and deep cycle of breathing by inhaling through your nose and exhaling through your mouth.

2. Focus your mind on relaxing, calming, or empowering thoughts.

3. Inhale for four seconds, filling your lungs and expanding your abdomen with air. Use a watch or clock with a second hand to help you keep a steady rhythm.

4. Hold your breath for four seconds (without tensing up).

5. Exhale for four seconds, getting rid of all your air.

6. Hold your breath for four seconds at the bottom of the breath. That is, hold your breath at the moment you run out of air.

7. Repeat this sequence six to eight times.

8. Repeat steps 1 through 7, but breathe and hold for six seconds.

9. Repeat steps 1 through 7, but breathe and hold for eight seconds.

This exercise may feel awkward, especially when you hold at the bottom of the breath. You may feel like you have to take a breath. Take a breath if you need to and keep practicing until it feels comfortable. Initially, you may want to inhale quickly after holding at the bottom of the breath. Over time you will be able to control your breath and keep the inhalations measured and smooth.

To bring this exercise to a close, let your breathing return to a normal pace. This happens naturally.

These techniques are adapted from *Superlearning 2000* by Ostrander and Schroeder (1994).

Practice

Breathe with the Music

This simple game will help you practice rhythmic delivery (pages 94–95). The game involves breathing and relaxation.

Key

Primary learning styles: auditory and kinesthetic
Domain: social-emotional development
Specific academic areas: applies to all
Educational bonus: ability to focus, self-regulation, positive self-concept, and improved circulation
Suggested music: slow classical music (sixty beats per minute)
Materials needed: music source

1. Play slow classical music (see the sample music lists on page 173).

2. As children watch, hug yourself and take a deep breath simultaneously.

3. Release your breath and the hug at the same time with a big smile.

4. Ask the children if they'd like to join you. (Some children will join you right away, others will want to watch, and others may present their own ideas.)

5. Repeat steps 2 and 3 with the children.

6. Ask the children, "What else could we do when we take a breath?"

This organic breathing game is great for easing transitions. For example, you could use this game when you move from outside play to inside play. Or you could use it when children finish lunch and are moving on to the next part of the day.

This game doubles as an affirmation exercise. While playing this game, I often start a conversation with the children by saying or asking the following:

- "I feel great. How do you feel?"

- "You are all champions. Did you know that? What is a champion?"

- "I love breathing. How does breathing make you feel?"

- "I love breathing with the music. How does the music make you feel?"

Practice

The Tree and the Wind

Note: Refer back to the Master Teaching Principles (part 1) for inspiration to ask questions, teach to all learning styles, improvise, and teach in width and depth while you play this game with children.

Key

Primary learning styles: all three learning styles are engaged

Domain: physical development

Specific academic area: science (identifying life cycles in plants and animals)

Educational bonus: early literacy (connecting letters with sounds and expanding vocabulary); early math (adding small groups); balance; and drama, role playing, and creativity

Suggested music: slow baroque or classical music (sixty beats per minute)

Materials needed: music source and your imagination

The Tree and the Wind can be used to calm children after they've been moving or to reinforce calm if they haven't been moving. Since this game relaxes children's bodies, eating lunch afterward is a great option. A relaxed body aids digestion.

The instructions for The Tree and the Wind are meant to serve only as a guide or a template. Please make this game your own and figure out how to play it best with your particular group of children.

1. With slow rhythmic music in the background, have the children stand up and pretend they are trees. Ask the children open-ended questions, rather than giving orders, while you pretend. For example, ask questions like these:

   - "If we're trees, what should our arms be?"

   - "What should our hands be?"

   - "What are roots?"

   - "Where do roots go?"

   You could also ask children to hug themselves as trees. This action helps children practice crossing the midline and helps them engage in positive affirmations. It also helps them explore which parts of their bodies (which parts of trees) could be affected by the environment.

2. Ask the children to help make wind sounds by breathing in through their noses and out through their mouths.

3. Ask the children, "What do trees need to grow?" or "What do trees drink?" or "What do trees eat?" The answers you receive will vary based on where the children live (urban versus rural) and what they have experienced. Honor children's differences and engage them in a joyful discussion that eventually leads to the answer, *water*. Discuss with the children how water helps trees grow. Talking about water can easily lead to a discussion about rain.

4. Lead the children in making the sound of rain by breathing in through your nose and out through your mouth. Encourage them to follow your lead and make the sounds themselves.

5. Ask children to become the rain with their bodies by using their hands and fingers. Demonstrate the falling rain by

moving your hands and fingers high above your head and then low to the ground. Continue this action with children as long as they let you, usually about ten to thirty seconds at first. As this game becomes a part of their routine, children will usually sustain the play for longer, which is evidence of increased mental focus and clarity.

6. Ask the children, "Where does rain come from?" The multitude of answers will make you smile and might even take your breath away. If you arrive at an answer of *clouds*, ask more questions to foster the development of critical-thinking skills:

   - "What color are the clouds when it rains?"

   - "What happens to the rain when the temerature drops from cold to freezing?"

   - "What other sounds do you hear during a storm?"

7. Repeat step 4. Have the children breathe in and out while making the sound of the rain, snow, or wind. Say to the children, "Doesn't it feel *wonderful* to drink water as a tree?" Introduce synonyms of *wonderful*, such as *fantastic, marvelous,* or *incredible.*

Don't feel that you need to end the game in an abrupt or overly planned manner. Many times the game ends naturally when children begin to sing a song or when it's time to play outside or eat lunch.

Variations
Once the children are used to this game as a part of their routine, extend their ability to focus by asking questions that encourage them to visualize how their trees interact with the environment:

- "Do animals visit the trees? What kind? What color? How many?"

- "What kinds of trees can you become? Can you become a cactus? A jungle tree? How about an apple tree or coconut tree?"

- "Can you count the animals or fruit?"

- "Can you add small groups of animals or fruit to see how many are in your tree?"

- "If it's raining, where do the animals go to keep dry? Where do these animals or fruits naturally exist? In the forest, desert, or jungle?"

- "How many different parts of the world can we visit?"

Practice

The Seed in the Ground

The Seed in the Ground is a variation of The Tree and the Wind (page 104). I use The Seed in the Ground when I work with children who are overly physical—prone to bumping and hitting each other with their tree branches!

Key

Primary learning styles: all three learning styles are engaged
Domain: cognitive development
Specific academic area: science (identifying life cycles in plants and animals)
Educational bonus: early literacy (positional words and expanded vocabulary), early math (sequencing), following directions, and creativity
Suggested music: slow early classical music (sixty beats per minute)
Materials needed: music source and your imagination

1. Ask the children to hold one hand in front of them with their palms facing the floor. Say, "Pretend your hand is the ground outside." If a child responds by saying, "That's not the ground, it's my hand," you can say, "You're right! It is your hand, but let's

pretend it's the ground outside!" If you smile and sound happy when you say this, you'll find this response works almost every time.

2. Continue by saying, "Now with your other hand, pick a seed." Model this action by picking an imaginary seed out of thin air. When you pick your seed out of the air, say something like, "Look, my seed is a flower seed, and my flower is blue!" (or any other color you like). Model the action and discovery, but don't tell the children how to respond (such as with the same flower or the same color). Multiple children, and eventually all of them, will chime in with, "Mine is red," "My flower is white," "My seed is a watermelon seed," and countless other types of seeds and colors. When children choose for themselves—the type of seed, the color of the plant, the kind of fruit, or whatever it is—they are visualizing this object and color. This is a big deal!

3. When everyone has a seed, say to the children, "Take your seed, put it on top of the ground, and push it down, down, down until the seed is under the ground." This can be a moment to use directional words for improved literacy skills. If you want, have everyone dig a hole for the seed before planting it.

4. Guide the children's thinking by asking, "I wonder what makes seeds grow?"

5. From this point on, the game is very similar to The Tree and the Wind. As a group, get to the word *rain* and then make the sound of rain with lots of breathing. Then use your free hand to act out the rain falling on the seed. Continue this action as long as they let you. After the rain, make the action of a seed slowly rising through the ground, usually portrayed by an index finger. Sometimes the seed needs more rain

to grow, which cycles the activity back to the sounds and actions of the rain.

Typically children want their flowers to keep growing until their entire bodies become the flowers, which eventually brings the game to a natural close. Consider the end of this game a transition to the next learning opportunity.

Of course, children can always react to games in unexpected ways. Once, while playing The Seed in the Ground, I noticed a little girl whimpering with her bottom lip sticking out. She was holding out her hand as the dirt, but her index finger, which was supposed to be the flower growing through the ground, was motionless under the ground. I asked her, "Is your seed growing?" She whimpered back, "Noo . . . noo." I asked the rest of the class to help by bringing more rain to her flower, and *they did*. The children gathered around the little girl and showered her with rain, which included both actions and sounds. The little girl looked happy and astonished. As she looked at the rain falling on her flower from the other children, her right hand inexplicably pushed her index finger through the ground. I think what she really needed was a little attention, but she also got the flower. Meanwhile, the rest of the class learned a great lesson in social-emotional development while practicing their breathing, which was effective and fun!

Variations

- A bee can visit the flowers to collect the nectar to make honey (science).

- The bee can fly above, to the side, or behind the flower (literacy).

- The bee can land on one, two, three, or more flower petals (math).

- The bee can share the flower's nectar with another bee (social-emotional development).

Practice

My Tree Was Cut Down!

This is another variation of The Tree and the Wind (page 104) that emerged from a child's unexpected improvisation (page 38). Four-year-old Pepito called out, "My tree was cut down!" during the game. Since then, I sometimes take this route myself, by design.

Key

Primary learning styles: all three learning styles are engaged

Domain: cognitive development

Specific academic area: science (identifying cycles of life)

Educational bonus: early literacy (comprehension and expanded vocabulary), early math (adding small groups), gross- and fine-motor skill development, and balance

Suggested music: early classical music (sixty beats per minute)

Materials needed: music source and a relatively soft floor

1. Begin playing The Tree and the Wind. Have the children become full-bodied trees and ask them what parts of a tree their body parts should represent.

2. Ask the children, "What do trees need to grow?" This discussion eventually leads to *rain,* which leads to more breathing techniques.

3. After you have started the cycle of rain and, perhaps, after animals visit the trees, exclaim, "My tree was just cut down!" You could use some other variation, such as "A storm blew down my tree!"

4. Lie down as a dead tree (most of the children will join you) and ask, "What do dead trees need to grow?" Children will share many ideas, such as sunlight and water. Eventually, you will likely arrive back to *rain.*

5. Make the sound of rain with the children. Little by little
   the trees will grow again.

Note: Repeat this game several times to help the children absorb the
concepts. Children usually find this game fun and humorous, so repeating it is usually a great choice. Sometimes I try to guide the game to a
discussion about the importance of trees in our world. I might ask a
question like, "Do trees help us?" Children usually respond with ideas
related to shade, giving fruit, and so forth. You might use this moment
to share the idea that trees give oxygen back to the air, which can lead
to more deep breathing. There are many great ways to come full circle
with this game!

Variations

With play-based activities, you can find moments to explore science.
I encourage you to use the term *circle of life* or *cycle of life* when you
play this version of The Tree and the Wind. For example, you could
say, "Wow, that was a cycle of life!" Some children may not be familiar
with the word *cycle*. You could explain it by saying, "A cycle is like a
circle. Let's make a circle with the rain." By doing so, children experience *cycle* in kinesthetic, visual, and auditory ways.

Practice

Eddie the Elephant

I love to use hand puppets
to introduce breathing to
toddlers, but this game
works beautifully with
preschoolers and kinder-
gartners as well. Don't be
afraid to improvise. The
puppet I use a lot is an
elephant named Eddie. I
have used the following

Key

Primary learning styles: visual and auditory
Domain: social-emotional development
Specific academic area: any a teacher chooses to
focus on
Educational bonus: cognitive development (breathing and relaxation), early literacy (synonyms and
descriptive words), identifying feelings, and building positive relationships
Suggested music: early classical music (sixty beats
per minute)
Materials needed: music source and a hand puppet

routine many times, and at some level, it has always worked in helping
young children breathe slowly, deeply, and smoothly. Use any puppet
you like, and you can name it whatever you like, Broom Hilda, Galileo,
or Enrique, for a few ideas. For the purpose of these instructions, let's
assume you're using an animal puppet of some kind.

1. Hide the puppet in a small container, such as a suitcase or in
   something with a zipper.

2. Pretend to hear a sound or sense movement from the hidden
   puppet in the container.

3. Ask the children if you should check to see what's inside the
   container.

4. Take a peek, show great surprise, and let the children know
   you saw an animal. (If some children show fear, tell them it's
   a very nice and happy animal.)

5. Take your time when peeking at the animal and act surprised
   each time. Children usually find this repetition humorous,

and it helps draw them into the activity emotionally. You can also use this moment as an opportunity to explore questions, such as "Should I give up?" or "Should I be brave?"

6. When the time seems right, pull the animal out of the container, but leave one of its legs trapped.

7. Introduce the animal by name and explain that it loves children. In the middle of your introduction, have the animal begin to panic. Help the children notice that its leg is caught.

8. Release the animal and bring it in close to you. Make the animal shake a little as if it is were crying. Ask the children, "Why is the elephant crying?"

9. After the children have answered the question, ask the elephant, "What would make you feel better?" Have the elephant whisper in your ear, and let the children know the elephant wants to breathe with his special music.

10. Put on slow early classical music (sixty beats per minute) and have the elephant breathe in and out with the music.

11. Have the elephant whisper in your ear. Share with the children that the elephant would like their help. Some children will not want to breathe with the elephant. Let the children know that whoever feels "big enough" can help the elephant. Many hesitant children will then join in the breathing.

12. Have the elephant whisper in your ear again. Let the children know the elephant would like them to breathe x number of times in a row. I usually use the numbers eleven, twelve, or thirteen because most children are fairly comfortable counting up to ten. Eleven, twelve, and thirteen might be new or confusing for them; this game can help them feel comfortable with these numbers.

13. Continue to play this game as long as children are engaged.

When you sense that the children are ready to move on, have Eddie whisper in your ear that he thinks it's time to do something else—play another game, eat lunch, play outside, or do something else. This is a natural way to bring the game to an end and begin something new.

Chapter 9

· · · · · · · · · · ·

Imagine or Visualize

Sometime in the middle of the fourth movement of his Ninth Symphony, the composer heard and felt every nuance of every phrase, the depth of each chord, and the foreshadowing of every gesture in more detail than anyone else in the concert hall. It was the premiere of what would be his final symphony. He was lost in his joy, and he was sharing that joy with others. The composer also expressed sadness through his music, which made the joy that much sweeter. The composer was experiencing the music in many ways simultaneously: cognitively, socially, emotionally, intellectually, physically, and spiritually. He conducted his symphony having heard the music thousands of times in his head. Unlike most composers, though, he had heard the music *only* in his head—because he was deaf. He could hear some sounds and feel vibrations, but he had never heard the clarity of the pitches or the timbre of the instruments in this symphony outside of his own mind. The composer was, of course, Ludwig van Beethoven.

This is, perhaps, one of the greatest examples of visualization or, as children call it, imagination. Visualization is not what we feel with our senses, but what images we experience in our minds. Beethoven used his practiced ability with visual mental imagery; that is, he used his mind's eye. The part of the human brain that engages when an architect visualizes a home design prior to drawing also engages when a scientist visualizes an equation before writing it down and when a composer hears music prior to writing the notes on staff paper.

According to Harvard professor and author Steven M. Kosslyn (1995), a strong connection exists between visual mental imagery and memory and spatial reasoning. In addition, visual mental imagery improves linguistic comprehension and motor-skill learning; this science supports the practice of athletes who visualize a skill to improve performance. Kosslyn also notes that many physicists, including Albert Einstein, confirm the connection between imagery and symbolic reasoning. In other words, when someone visualizes, they are, in fact, reconstructing information stored in their memory for use in the present. Visualization can improve our abilities in many areas, including memory, reasoning, and perception.

Visualization—or imagination—is an activity that connects the *art of being* with the *science of doing* (page 6). For a composer like Beethoven, visualization was the birth of a composition, the beginning of a song, the first note of a phrase. Creating is a powerful thing and can be a life-changing event. For those of us who do it often, creating becomes a way of life.

Visualizing in Sports

In sports psychology, visualization is an effective tool for improving overall performance. Olympic teams, including in the United States and Canada, are much more likely to use psychologists when preparing for the Olympics than they were a decade or two ago. The simple effort of visualizing your performance or action can have an amazing effect. Harvard-trained psychologist Dr. Stephen Kraus (2006) states, "Today, research in sports psychology has made it clear that visualization can enhance success and performance in sports. But parallel research in positive psychology has confirmed that visualization can enhance success in everyday life, making it a valuable tool for those interested in motivation, self-help, and self-improvement. But the reasons that visualization enhances the psychology of success are more practical and pragmatic than followers of Freudian psychology or popular self-help movements would have us believe." Dr. Kraus goes on to discuss how visualization enhances confidence, boosts motivation, and is an important form of practice. The proven effectiveness of visualization supports its use in sports and other areas, such as in the early childhood classroom.

The *art of being* has foundations in affirmation. The *science of doing* has foundations in visualization. The success of the Swiss ski team at the 1972 Olympics is a great example of the power of visualization. In preparation for the Olympics, the Swiss ski team utilized visualization in a new way. After scouting the ski run for the coming Olympics, a member of the Swiss team skied the run with a small movie camera mounted to his helmet. The camera captured the run from the skier's point of view. Later the entire team met in a room with a projector and watched footage of that ski run over and over until every detail was committed to memory. The trainers then pushed the Swiss team even further and instructed them to practice an intense form of visualization. The team used breathing techniques to slow their heart rates to about sixty beats per minute, and then they used their minds to visualize the ski route they had just watched on film. Examine the Swiss team's records for the 1964, 1968, and 1972 Winter Olympics on the table below. The success of this visualization work is clear.

	1964	1968	1972
Men's downhill	4th place	Bronze medal and 10th place	Gold and silver medals with four of the top six finishers
Men's giant slalom	4th place	Silver medal and 7th place	Silver and bronze medals
Women's downhill	17th place	7th place	Gold medal
Women's giant slalom	9th place	Bronze medal	Gold medal

The work of the Swiss ski team revolutionized the use of visualization in sports training. Many accomplished athletes in golf, baseball, tennis, and other sports now use visualization as one of many training tools to enhance performance.

Reaping the Benefits of Visualization

Beethoven and the Swiss ski team used visualization, but athletes and musicians are not the only ones who actively use this technique. Anyone in any field can and should use it. A great chef, for example, concocts a dish mentally before stepping into a kitchen. A film director sees each shot in the mind's eye before a single actor walks on set. An artist visualizes an image before putting a brush to the canvas. A novelist often knows how a book will end before writing the first sentence. A custodian visualizes a map of the buildings before cleaning begins. Visualization can even be applied to everyday situations. Have you ever lost something and retraced your steps in your mind's eye to find it? This is a form of visualization. To see things in the mind's eye is to see things like a child. We must stop living with mundane energy and start seeing things as we want them to be, like a child would. When this practice becomes part of our routine, we can achieve a higher level of performance and a higher state of being.

Visualization exercises the brain in ways that push it out of survival mode and into a creative mode. This technique can also generate self-fulfilling images that lead to a powerful self-concept. When we visualize our success in a particular area over and over again and make efforts to achieve that vision, confidence increases.

Visualization works with adults and helps them succeed in various ways. Can preschool children practice visualization the same way adults do? The answer is no. Children should practice visualization, but only in developmentally appropriate ways—think *imagination*.

Using (Losing?) Imagination

You can help develop strong and happy children. Give children who use their imagination free rein to be creative and guide children who don't. There are plenty of reasons why some children use their imagination less than others. Technology, for example, sometimes creates situations where young children don't need to use their imagination. Children who watch a lot of television or play hours of video games have visual and auditory cues given to them, decreasing opportunities to imagine things on their own.

As a society, we expect to be entertained rather than entertain ourselves. Compare today's children to children only a few decades ago. These children did not have televisions or video games. They had radios. For entertainment, the family gathered around the radio. They'd hear a voice and a story, but they'd have to imagine the rest. Before the radio, there were only books. Readers have to imagine what characters sound like and look like. Reading a book takes more brain power than watching a movie. Children who are entertained by technology have fewer reasons to use their imagination.

In general, children use their imagination less often today than children did fifty years ago. Of course, many variables impact how often children use their imagination, such as personality, level of parenting, and overall environment. It is our responsibility, not only as teachers and parents but also as a generation of adults, to guide children in ways that encourage them to develop and use their imagination.

Imagination is key to children's overall growth. As teachers, we can make sure imagination is a part of children's daily routine. What follows are ways children and adults can use visual imagery, visualization, and imagination to think in abstract ways.

Engaging Children in Visualization

Once we realize that visualization connects the *art of being* (knowing who you are and why you exist) with the *science of doing* (accomplishing things in real-life situations), we must ask ourselves, "What is the simplest way to engage children's imagination?" A mentor once asked me this question. I had to think about it and talk about it for a long time. After observing great early childhood educators and after playing with children myself, I finally came up with an answer. The answer is simple but not always easy for adults. In order to engage children's imagination, we need to ask children questions, involve them in games, and encourage their free play—even if it unnerves us. We must ask children open-ended questions, be patient enough to listen, and take time to have real conversations with them.

I often use an abstract guessing game with children to encourage their imagination. Before the game Twenty Questions became popular in the 1940s, it existed in many simple versions. I offer a simple version of Twenty Questions in the practice section of this chapter. When you analyze my version, called Three Guesses (page 121), you'll find it does more than simply entertain. It engages the creative parts of the brain because it requires visualization. In addition, the game impacts self-concept in a positive way because it encourages children to discover and figure out something on their own.

Goal setting is another fundamental "game" that can improve visualization and strengthen self-concept. I don't mean the kind of goal setting where you set a goal, write it down, and then think about how you'll never reach it. Successful goal setting is a type of visualization and requires imagination. Many people make the mistake of thinking that goal setting is simply wishing for something to happen. Instead, think of goal setting as visualizing the feeling of *already having achieved the goal*. This type of visualization engages the brain in ways that lead to actions that support the goal. You can play goal-setting games with young children by having them draw, talk, and write about things they want to do and be in the future.

Visualizing the Possibilities

Imagination is powerful. Using it puts you in the realm of champions, which is a magical place. Imagination leads to *possibility thinking,* and possibility thinking leads to creating, inventing, and leading. Being a *possibility thinker* means being able to get back up from a low moment with visualization and affirmation. Become a possibility thinker and you could become addicted to the sensation of creating. Once you have had the experience of creating, you will find it very hard to go back to only consuming.

Let's keep imagination alive in our children by using visualization with children and ourselves as often as we can. In this way, we can begin to live like children and guide children in ways that help them think for themselves.

Practice

Three Guesses

I started playing this game with my son, Nicky, when he was about four years old. It's very similar to the well-known game called Twenty Questions. We call our version Three Guesses.

Key

Primary learning style: auditory
Domain: cognitive development
Specific academic area: literacy (language development)
Educational bonus: deductive reasoning, expanded vocabulary, and critical thinking
Suggested music: none
Materials needed: brain power

This game is simple, and it encourages visualization and imagination in linear and abstract ways. My son is now twelve. First I'll explain how we play Three Guesses now that he is older; then I'll describe how you can adapt it for preschoolers.

Playing with Older Children

1. Nicky likes to go first, so he chooses a person, a place, or an object (anyone, anywhere, or anything in the universe). He lets me know when he has made his choice. If Nicky feels generous, he picks a person, which is the least difficult category to guess. He chooses a place if he wants a more difficult category and a thing if he wants to stump me. He chooses a thing most often.

2. Then I ask the first question, which is always the same, "Is it a person, place, or thing?"

3. Then I ask Nicky any yes-or-no question I think will lead me to the answer:

   • My most typical question for the category of person is, "Do I know this person?"

   • Typical questions for places include, "Have I been there?" "Does this place exist on planet Earth?" and "Is this place somewhere in the ocean?"

   • Questions for things are various, because they really could be *anything*. Once, Nicky chose the word *the* as the thing. (I didn't win.)

4. I sometimes ask for help in the form of clues. Usually we limit this option to three clues, but this number is negotiable. The clues encourage deductive reasoning, abstract thinking, problem-solving skills, and critical-thinking skills.

5. I can ask an unlimited number of questions, but I can only make three guesses to identify the correct answer.

6. When the game ends, we switch roles and Nicky becomes the guesser.

Playing with Preschoolers

1. When you play this game with preschoolers, choose something or someone they know. An animal or familiar object might work best to start.

2. Instead of asking, "Is it a person, place, or thing?" guide children by saying something like, "I'm thinking of an animal. Can you guess what color it is or where it lives?" Over time, children will begin to ask questions without guidance. This game might be too abstract for some young children at first, but introducing children to abstract thinking early on is important.

3. Offer clues if you see children struggling or looking frustrated. Don't wait for them to ask for clues.

4. Allow children unlimited questions and more than three guesses.

5. When children guess the animal or object correctly, have that object or animal (in the form of a hand puppet, for example) handy for children to play with. Giving the object to children is a nice way to transition into another activity or free-play time.

Practice

Calling upon Memories

This exercise is for adults and children. It will help you and the children exercise your brains, specifically the part you use for visualization. During the activity,

you will re-create memories that are comforting, calming, or empowering in your mind. More than just an act of remembering, the exercise will help you reconnect with the mind-set you had in those moments. This simple exercise can double as a calming and affirming activity.

Memories that employ the senses (sight, sound, smell, touch, and so on) are especially useful in this exercise. I like to recall my grandmother—my nana—making tortillas when I was a boy. I remember how she looked at the stove and how the tortillas, coffee, and refried beans smelled in the air. These three scents and the image of my nana in the room carry me to a place of stress-free living and joy.

You, of course, have many memories. Some memories come from experiences involving family, good friends, accomplishments, and trips. Some memories are from your adult life and others are from high school or elementary school. For example, I remember making a film with my fourth-grade class and going to see the film at a film festival with all of my schoolmates. I remember the great feeling of achievement in that moment.

For Adults

Here's what I'd like you to try yourself:

1. Choose a memory. Don't overthink it. Let the memory come to you instinctively.

2. Find a memory that makes you smile or feel peaceful, powerful, or free. If the memory doesn't make you feel happy, choose another.

3. Focus on the memory and try to remember as many details as possible.

4. Recall the sensory elements associated with the memory, such as smells, tastes, colors, sounds, and feelings.

5. Try to see and feel the memory from your perspective.

6. Try to see and feel the memory from others' perspectives.

7. As you continue to focus on the memory, begin a gentle cycle of breathing.

8. To finish, stretch, breathe, and think about what you want to do next in your life.

You can wrap up this exercise by writing out your goals for your professional or personal life.

For Children
Here's how you might try this exercise with children:

1. Ask children to close their eyes and use their imagination.

2. Ask them to think of something good that has happened to them. Guide the children by telling them that the moment may have happened yesterday or last week or maybe a long time ago. Remind them that the memory should be something that makes them happy.

3. Ask children questions and give them prompts for exploring their memory deeply:

   • "Remember the place you were. Where are you? What is it like?"

- "Who is there? Imagine these people in your mind. What do they look like? What are they wearing?"

- "What smells do you remember? What do they smell like?"

- "Do you remember any special sounds? What are they?"

- "What is happening that makes you happy? How do you feel?"

Practice

Eagle in the Sky

This visualization exercise for children helps them practice seeing things from a different perspective, from a bird's-eye view. You can improvise to create many variations to this game. Here is the version I like to play:

Key

Primary learning style: kinesthetic
Domain: cognitive development
Specific academic area: science (identifying animals and plants in nature)
Educational bonus: thinking from different perspectives and literacy (expanded vocabulary)
Suggested music: early classical music (sixty beats per minute)
Materials needed: imagination

1. Play either slow classical music or relaxing music that includes sounds of nature.

2. Invite the children to become birds with their entire bodies.

3. Ask the children questions about what they see.

4. When they respond, ask them questions of depth. For example, if the children say, "I see my mommy," you could ask, "What is she wearing?" or "What is she doing?" At the

beginning of this activity, children's perspective—what they see in their mind as they pretend—will be similar to their everyday perspective.

5. To guide them to think about a different point of view, ask the children to fly up high. Continue to ask them questions about what they see from the sky when they look down. You may need to guide them further by asking questions like, "Do you see a lake or do you see the top of a house?"

6. If you want, incorporate breathing to make the sound of the wind rushing by.

7. Continue this game until you sense that the children want to move on.

To end the game, I often transition to reading either a book about nature or a book that uses different perspectives. I often read *Giraffes Can't Dance* by Giles Andreae, which contains images of a giraffe walking into the distance and a cricket up close.

Variations

- If a child asks to be another animal, such as a bear, ask all the children to become that animal and take a different journey. You might climb to the top of a mountain and find a great vista!

- Ask the children to use a part of their bodies to represent an eagle far away. Children often use their fingers or hands to represent the eagle at a distance. Then ask the children to use their bodies to look like the eagle when it's really close. Children often become full-bodied eagles.

- Use this visualization game to transition to a play-based breathing game. Tell the children, as eagles, that the wind is picking up. Make the sound of the wind with the children and then the sound of rain. Then make the sound of a storm complete with the sounds of thunder.

Practice

What Color Is Your Bird?

This activity is a variation of The Tree and the Wind (page 104). The key to success with this game is how you ask the question "What color is your bird?"

Key

Primary learning styles: all three learning styles are engaged

Domain: physical development

Specific academic area: science (identifying animals and plants in nature)

Educational bonus: thinking from different perspectives and literacy (expanded vocabulary)

Suggested music: early classical music (sixty beats per minute)

Materials needed: imagination and music

1. Start The Tree and the Wind game and establish a cycle of breathing.

2. With slow rhythmic music in the background, have the children stand up and pretend they are trees.

3. Ask the children, "What do trees need to grow?" Follow the discussion until it naturally leads to *rain*. Lead children in making the sound of rain by breathing in through your nose and out through your mouth.

4. When the rain subsides, tell the children that a bird is visiting your tree and say, "My bird is red." (Any color will do.) Then say nothing. Children will usually respond with things like, "My bird is blue," "My bird is black," "My bird is red," "My bird is a rainbow," or even "My bird is invisible."

5. Acknowledge the children with your eyes, individually and as a group. Let them all speak simultaneously. Teaching children to raise their hands and to take turns is a great idea for another time. During this game, however, don't stop the creative flow of ideas.

6. Have the rain return and lead the children in more breathing. Ask the children, "Where should the birds go so they don't get wet?" You will hear many answers, but eventually you'll hear, "In the tree!"

7. When the birds seek shelter in the tree, I often ask, "How many birds are hiding in your tree?" Sometimes I follow with, "I wonder how many birds are in my tree and Katie's tree together." You can then count the birds as a group.

8. End the activity by asking the trees to give themselves a "tree hug." You might also say, "Give your brains a kiss for a job well done."

By letting children pick their own color for their bird, you encourage them to create, to self-regulate, and to visualize. When they say the color of their bird, their brain sees the color; it is a simple but powerful way to help children develop.

Practice

The Magic Bag

The Magic Bag is a simple kinesthetic visualization game. During the game, children use touch to identify objects hidden in bags. Consider making or buying cloth bags with drawstrings to use over and over again.

> **Key**
>
> **Primary learning style:** kinesthetic
> **Domains:** cognitive development and language development
> **Specific academic areas:** applies to all
> **Educational bonus:** math (shapes and counting objects) and literacy (vocabulary development)
> **Suggested music:** none
> **Materials needed:** objects, such as shapes, small animals, spoons, and so on, and opaque bags

1. Put one object in each bag. For young children, start with things that have simple shapes, such as squares and triangles, or objects the children know, such as trucks, dolls, hats, or markers.

2. Show the children a bag. Put your hand in the bag and guess what is inside.

3. Then have the children feel the object in the bags without looking inside. Guide the children by asking questions, such as "Is your object hard or soft?" "Is it a shape or an animal?" Focus on the guessing process. Make sure children are encouraged to explore and guess over and over again.

4. After a child guesses, open the bag to see if the guess is correct.

5. Over time, gradually increase the complexity and variety of the objects you use.

A nice way to transition from this game to another is to have a puppet, such as Eddie the Elephant (page 112), hidden in a larger bag. Have the children guess what is in this larger bag. Finding Eddie the Elephant will create a natural transition to the breathing game.

Chapter 10

· · · · · · · · · · ·

Move

The good news is that children have lots of energy. What's the bad news? There isn't any if you help children use their energy, rather than try to control it. You cannot control children. Some teachers think otherwise and end up spending a lot of time and effort herding children. A stern taskmaster can certainly corral children, but when the controlling entity is not present, children will likely erupt with chaotic energy in response.

Sometimes children's energy has to be directed, especially when it comes to safety issues. Most of the time, though, effective and masterful teachers can engage children's energy in ways that foster creative and joyful learning. Movement helps children learn and burn energy at the same time; it can have fantastic results.

Moving and Self-Regulating

How do the finest early childhood teachers guide children? Surprisingly, they don't use the word *no* a lot. They sometimes use *stop* or *freeze*, but not often. If you tell children to stop or freeze, you'll likely observe a range of reactions: one child might show difficulty being still, and another child might refuse (or be unable) to stay still at all. By telling a child what to do, especially in a serious tone, you are imposing your will and structure on that child. In situations where control is imposed, you'll often find attitudes of rebellion. Control and rebellion are connected. One is an action, and the other is its consequence. Children need structure and guidance—as do adults—but how much, what kind, and when?

The specific language we use with young children is powerful. I picked up a "magic word" from Rick Wamer, world-class mime and modern dance artist. The word is *hold*, as in "Hold your energy." When you ask children to hold their energy, you provide options: whether or not to hold, how to hold, and how long to hold. The phrase "Hold your energy" often works like a charm for children. With it, you can harness children's natural tendency to move and use it as a vehicle for learning. Use this phrase the next time you're with children. In the middle of playing or dancing with them, say, "Hold your energy!" Demonstrate holding as you say it, and then hold with joy. Notice the reactions from the children. I often see reactions of self-discovery and expressions of having fun. When you couple this technique with literacy and math strategies, you have a game that encourages self-regulation, creative thinking, critical thinking, and social-emotional development, along with academic readiness. The words *hold* and *energy* are powerful.

Encouraging self-regulation is a preventive and positive way to approach discipline. The only kind of discipline that really sticks is self-discipline. External discipline becomes a power struggle between adults and children; self-discipline prevents this challenge entirely. In addition, self-regulation is empowering because it involves individual choice. When children choose for themselves, they feel empowered and trusted and will begin to take risks in learning situations. For these reasons, many of the games and techniques in this book are designed to help children use their own energy and make choices. Some adults think that teaching self-regulation means teaching children not to move. Ironically, the opposite is true. We need movement to teach self-regulation!

Moving for Physical Heath

Exercise is healthy. When children engage in movement games, they are telling their bodies and minds that exercise is fun. In light of the current obesity epidemic in children around the world, making exercise a part of children's daily routine is vital. The International Obesity Task Force estimates that worldwide 22 million children under five are overweight or obese (Cosgrove-Mather 2002). In the United States, approximately 60 percent of adults and nearly 32 percent of children are overweight or obese. In some countries, more than 30 percent of children ages seven to eleven are overweight or obese (Lobstein, Rigby, and Leach 2005). In Egypt, more than 25 percent of four-year-olds are overweight. In Chile, Peru, and Mexico, more than 25 percent of children between the ages of four and ten are overweight.

In 2004 the Office of Head Start supported the I Am Moving, I Am Learning project, which recommends children play at vigorous or moderate levels for an accumulated sixty minutes every day. Making movement a part of children's daily routine is what's most important. In 2002 the National Association for Sport and Physical Education (NASPE) published a call to action titled *Active Start* (2002). The report recommends that toddlers accumulate at least thirty minutes of planned physical play on a daily basis. According to Loraine Elizabeth Parish and Mary E. Rudisill, proponents of the High Autonomy Physical Play Environment (HAPPE) program, "an inadequate movement foundation in the early years puts children at risk for becoming inactive, overweight—or even obese—adults who may develop coronary heart disease, diabetes mellitus, and/or other chronic illnesses" (Parish and Rudisill 2006, 1). The HAPPE program strives to motivate and engage toddlers in physical play that builds basic motor skills that become the foundation for a lifetime of healthy activity.

Even the National Football League (NFL) has taken the call to promote fitness for children. The NFL partnered with the American Heart Association to create the NFL Play 60 Challenge (American

Heart Association 2010). The program strongly encourages children to get sixty minutes of physical activity a day. The program helps schools encourage physically active lifestyles throughout the year by providing classroom and school-wide resources.

Moving and Learning in Many Ways

When moving with children in learning situations, take advantage of the many opportunities to interact with them physically and verbally. Which movements work best with particular music, how words relate to music, and how all of it makes you feel are subjective. One child may think certain music suggests a certain action. Don't hesitate to weave that child's ideas into the fabric of the game. Encourage children to expand how they express themselves; movement can be an interactive and engaging means of expression for all learners:

- Kinesthetic learners are naturally inclined—and invited—to learn in this manner.

- Visual learners are invited because movement games are highly visual.

- Auditory learners are invited when you verbalize the words and movements being shared.

You can create lifelong learners through movement:

- Learning through movement increases comprehension, especially for kinesthetic learners but also for visual and auditory learners.

- Movement games that involve balance help children develop physically, build self-confidence, practice delayed gratification, and improve decision-making, self-regulation, and leadership skills.

• Movement enhances emotional intelligence when children use their bodies to express emotions. For children who express themselves openly, movement is an ideal outlet. For children who are reticent, movement offers a new way to begin to express themselves. Using movement to express emotion helps all children develop social-emotional skills.

Movement games excite young children about learning and encourage them to think for themselves, to improve their academic performance, and to become healthier. Of course, you must embrace movement and improved health as well. As guides, we must challenge ourselves to be the best role models of health we can be. Teachers should play the movement games too!

Moving toward Literacy Development

The phrase *hold your energy* is central to the action of Energy Dance (page 139). This game will improve children's literacy skills—expanding vocabulary and comprehension—while also addressing social-emotional development. In the game, children become objects, words, and emotions with their bodies while moving to music from all over the world. When children create the word *big* with their bodies, they understand the word *big* because they become it. From there, exploring synonyms— becoming the words *huge* or *gigantic,* for example—is a natural step. Vocabularies can expand through movement in an effective, developmentally appropriate, and joyful way.

When I play Energy Dance with children, I use lots of antonyms or synonyms. I've found that having a list of words readily available— both in my head and in writing—helps me make sure I'm building children's vocabulary over time. By having a list, I can ensure I'm not repeating the same words over and over again. Instead, I'm giving children new words to express themselves. Although this game is teacher directed, asking children questions about how the music makes them feel is important. Giving children an opportunity to share their ideas will increase their ownership of this learning experience. When you first start playing this game, you'll find the words that children offer are simple. As you introduce new words, their suggestions will become more complex. Eventually, as your list of synonyms grows, you might even learn some new words yourself! I also use this game to introduce other languages to children, specifically my second language, Spanish.

Moving toward Complexity

Making movement a part of children's daily activities is important. Finding learning opportunities that utilize children's abundant energy is a must. As you work on vocabulary with children, increase the complexity of words over time. Start with object words and then expand to emotional words. For example, begin by saying to children, "Let's become a ball with our bodies!" or "Become a triangle with two of your friends!" *Ball* and *triangle* are simple and concrete words. From there, you can increase the complexity while still using object-based words. For example, introduce the words *huge, gigantic,* or *massive* to describe the ball, and ask children to become the new words with their bodies.

Eventually, you can increase the complexity of the game by using emotions. Becoming the word *happy* is pretty simple, but how does that term differ from *excited* or *thrilled*? With this kind of game, you increase children's vocabulary while also giving them new ways to express increasingly complex concepts and emotions.

You can add movement and complexity to activities generally considered sedentary. After you read a book to young children, you could invite them to become the characters in the book. Often children will do this naturally. For example, consider the book *Jazzy in the Jungle* by Lucy Cousins. In the story, baby Jazzy—a baby lemur—plays hide-and-seek with his mother. The baby hides so well that the mother cannot find her baby, and she begins a wider search for him. She searches the jungle asking, "Where are you?" which is followed by the response "Not here" by many animals. Eventually the mother finds the baby with the help of the other jungle animals. It is an excellent early reader book.

This story provides a lot of options for movement. To start, you could ask, "Where do you think baby Jazzy is hiding?" which will lead to movement connected to decision making. If multiple children are playing together, you will see some children begin to lead others; leadership is first experienced in play. At first, most children will want to find Jazzy very quickly. Over time and acting as a guide, you can increase the number of animals that the mother asks before she finds her baby. By increasing the number of animals, you provide a safe and fun way for children to experience delayed gratification, which also contributes to improved self-regulation. You can also make the search longer and more challenging by introducing other obstacles, such as mountains, lakes, or volcanoes. By finding success at the end of each search, you reinforce children's self-confidence in an engaging, play-based manner.

As early childhood expert Mimi Chenfield would say, ask yourself the question, "What else?" What else can you create? How much can you help others create? As teachers, we can guide young children to be critical thinkers by asking questions and allowing them to enter into a discussion with us. It's that simple. It's very powerful. But it's not always easy.

Moving, Visualizing, and Acting

You can change simple movement games into more complex games by adding visualization and music. I have had the great pleasure of working with Dr. Carroll Rinehart. Carroll has been very successful in facilitating student-created operas all over the United States. Taking a cue from him, I now direct student-created musicals as a part of my weekly work with children. While there are some differences between musicals and operas, there are many similarities. Creating a musical is a process rich in literacy development. It helps children increase their vocabulary and improve their comprehension, reading, and writing skills. This organic, joy-filled process is also filled with wonderful opportunities for social-emotional development, helping children practice confidence, cooperation, and sharing.

In the last few years, I have codirected student-created musicals at Ochoa Elementary, a public elementary school in Tucson, Arizona. Ochoa Elementary is an amazing school. All classes, from preschool through fifth grade, are Reggio-inspired and emphasize a holistic, joyful, and process-based approach to learning. I, with fourth- and fifth-graders at Ochoa Elementary, produced a musical adaptation of *Snow White and the Seven Dwarfs*, which I wrote about in chapter 3 (page 35). The students created the entire script and much of the staging themselves; student-created musicals are indeed student created. Movement was an important part of producing this particular musical. Each song included either a dance or some other gross-motor activity. The students also moved a lot as they acted out scenes. Movement played a key role in the children's ability to learn, absorb, and remember the elements of the musical. Each musical is a journey for the children and the teachers. The process fosters children who want to be at school and who see school as a place to create and learn.

While there are many ways to encourage children's intellectual, physical, social, emotional, and spiritual growth, using movement is one of the most critical ways. As Mimi Chenfeld says, children have a "magic vocabulary" made up of the things that most interest them. For most children, at least part of the magic vocabulary includes moving, shaking, twisting, hopping, skipping, and other types of movement. It is our responsibility as teachers to create lifelong learners. Using movement is one of the best ways to accomplish this.

Practice

Energy Dance

Play this game with children to improve their literacy skills, as well as to develop their social-emotional skills. You can play this game in many different ways. It's simple and allows you and the children to let go and express yourselves physically and emotionally.

I am not a kinesthetic learner by nature, but I've improved a lot in this area through practice; I can now express myself with gestures and movements more comfortably. In other words, if I can play this game, so can you.

Key

Primary learning styles: kinesthetic and auditory
Domain: language development
Specific academic area: literacy
Educational bonus: gross- and fine-motor skill development, social-emotional development, and creativity
Suggested music: music from around the world, including jazz, classical, folk, and gypsy music
Materials needed: music source

1. Turn on the music. You can choose any kind of music, but consider using this game to introduce children to different countries with music from all over the world. (This is something Mimi Chenfeld taught me.) Here is a list of possible selections, but don't feel limited to these:

   - salsa and merengue (Latin America, including Cuba and Puerto Rico)

   - blues (Southern United States and African American cultures)

   - swing (United States)

   - folk songs (Russia, Mexico, and Spain, among many others)

- koto drumming (Japan)

- gypsy music (Hungary, Spain, and France, among others)

- romantic-era classical music (France, Germany, Austria, and Hungary, among others)

- marches (United States)

- soundtracks from movies (various countries)

2. With music in the background, lead the children in moving to the music. It's okay if you don't have a dance background, because specific steps are not necessary. Remember to be respectful and to honor children's different personalities. Some children may want to watch before they feel comfortable moving or dancing.

3. Ask about and discuss the music in general terms. You might say, for example, "This music sounds smooth." Then become the word *smooth* with your body. You can start by just using your face to become the word, and then add your arms and hands. Eventually, use your entire body to become the word. This activity sounds abstract because it is! Abstract thinking is a skill we should encourage in young children.

   - While you move to the music, many words may come to mind. Share these words with the children. In addition, ask the children, "What does this music make you feel like?" Children of all ages can come up with word choices. Young children will come up with simple words, so be ready with plenty of synonyms to help expand their vocabulary. Here are some common words used in this game:

low	lower	lowest
high	higher	highest
happy	excited	surprised
energetic	wonderful	fantastic
incredible	marvelous	jumpy

Here are some additional ideas for playing this game:

- If you find a word that the children love to represent, use that word and its synonyms frequently.

- Keep a running list of words used to assist children who are visual learners.

- If a word can become part of a rhyme or song, sing the word to enhance learning and nurture a love for learning.

- Use a variety of music from around the globe. Use this as an opportunity to explore different cultures.

- Be respectful and honor the different love languages in your room. Give affirmations in ways that communicate to various personalities.

To end the game, you could engage the children in reflective dialogue. We often take time for reflective dialogue with adults, but children are just as expressive. Children are often ready to chill and chat about an activity after it is complete. As guides of young children, let's be careful not to underestimate their abilities.

Chapter 11

· · · · · · · · · · ·

Add Dramatic Delivery

To guide young children, we desperately need to start with one thing—their attention. We must gain their attention before we can even begin to help them develop. We have to compete with televisions, computers, and handheld games for children's attention every day. I use the term *dramatic delivery* to describe a technique for gaining children's attention. Needless to say, dramatic delivery involves drama. Games involving dramatic delivery are often accompanied by fast music with a tempo of 120 beats per minute. Examples of dramatic delivery include using bingo, card games, role playing, and the games and techniques in this book while exploring topics with children. It is critical for those of us in the field of early childhood education to be joyous, funny, and, yes, dramatic.

Surfing the Words (page 146) is an exercise in dramatic delivery. The technique helps children fall in love with reading and storytelling. It combines the rhythmic energy of music and spoken words to immerse children in a total experience. This technique also offers teachers an opportunity to open up—to embrace the emotion of the music and to let it guide a reading. When playing Surfing the Words, mimic the music with your voice as you read by adjusting your volume, pace, and inflection. Make sure the music is loud enough to be an integral part of the auditory experience but not so loud that it's overpowering.

Children's responses during Surfing the Words have been various, ranging from joy and laughter to quiet focus. Teachers who have used the technique have noticed the results. Head Start teacher Donna Swartz of Coshocton, Ohio, reports the following:

> The first time I read with the music, one little boy who had never listened to a story sat mesmerized. After the story, he remembered every detail! He was even observed retelling or rereading the story. As I progressed at Surfing the Words, the children seemed to grasp more and more.

Surfing the Words is one way of going beyond a simple reading of a book. *Going beyond* means using the book as a platform for learning many things. After a child knows and loves any story, use that story to focus on specific literacy, math, science, or social-emotional skills. For the skilled teacher focused on process rather than outcome, this occurs organically.

Parents have also reacted favorably to the use of dramatic delivery through Surfing the Words. A parent whose daughter attends the Head Start program where Donna Swartz teaches describes this scene:

> My daughter Natasha was having a hard time recognizing her letters and sitting still while being read to. Her Head Start teachers started using these [Surfing the Words] techniques in the classroom with her, and I was using them at home with her as well. It was not very long before she was sitting still while being read to. Not long after that she started pointing to letters in the book that were in her name and saying "That's in my name; it's the letter *N*." She would tell me what the letter was. As a teacher and parent, I have seen children who could not sit still for a story progress to being able to sit and be interested in the story being read.

Surfing the Words is about finding joy in reading and about telling a story with emotion. When surfing, start out with early classical
or baroque music because it has patterns that are easy to predict. The
patterns allow the reader to think ahead to match changes in volume,
pace, and inflection. Early classical music has many inherent qualities
that are ideal for early brain development, including rich frequencies.
Additionally, early classical and baroque music are relaxing and calming, which helps children absorb what they are learning and remain
focused for longer periods. Dive right into this activity; there is no such
thing as a perfect surf, only varying levels of effectiveness. The more
you surf, the more you and the children will enjoy the ride.

The ideal time to play Surfing the Words, and activities like it, is
after relaxation and breathing exercises. Use the directions for Surfing
the Words as a template or guide, tailoring the game to your needs.
For example, you can use Surfing the Words to focus on math, science,
literacy, or social-emotional development, depending on your needs. By
choosing the appropriate book, you can address any topic. Based on the
content of the book and your ability to take tangents, you can address
any domain in a play-based manner. The music engages children and
increases their emotional involvement, which increases their interest.
Asking questions and improvising will come in handy, but try to focus
on one major domain and several subcategories within that domain per
reading.

Just as Surfing the Words allows variety, so do the symphony games
(pages 148–52). In musical terms, *symphony* refers to a specific form
and convention that composers use. I use the term differently in the
context of early childhood education. The symphony games that follow
encourage children to use their bodies to become emotions, seasons, or
environments, such as the weather, water, animals, and plants on an
island. Just as symphonies connect layers of sound, these early childhood symphonies connect layers of learning, making the experience
both exciting and meaningful for children.

Practice

Surfing the Words

If you don't feel comfortable improvising in this activity, read the book with the music in advance to find places where you can use volume, pace, and inflection. You might come up with special voices for the different characters in the story. Have fun using this technique with children. The more fun you have, the more engaged the children will be.

1. Share with the children that you have an exciting book to read to them. Start the music.

2. Throughout the activity, take every opportunity to affirm the children. Keep comments in the present tense, such as "You can all read so well!"

3. Find opportunities to teach specific letters and letter sounds from the book in auditory, kinesthetic, and visual ways.

4. Surf the words! Read the story and change the volume, pace, and inflection of your voice to match the music. Pay attention to the emotion of the story line, and remind yourself that you can speak softly with great emotion. Some of the best moments occur when the music is soft and the drama of the story is intense.

5. As you read, consider extending the exercise in one or more of the following ways. Continue matching the music and stay engaged emotionally.

- Emphasize the idea of reading from left to right.

- Have the children repeat selected words and the beginning consonants of selected words in time with the music.

- Have the children repeat any patterns or rhymes.

6. When the story ends, change the music to slow classical music (sixty beats per minute) or turn it off entirely. Then ask children questions about what happened in the story, which will lead to a retelling of the story.

Variations

As an extension, use classical music from a more recent period, such as the romantic era. Romantic-era music is wonderful to use, but it will keep you on your toes because its tempo and emotion fluctuate in unpredictable ways. This fluctuation is the main difference between classical music of the romantic era and music of the early classical or baroque era. I've used music that frequently changes moods in this activity, including music by Tchaikovsky, Copland, Rachmaninoff, Mahler, Beethoven, and Respighi, among others. Here are some examples of romantic-era music I find effective. I've matched the music to books as a place to start:

Book	Suggested Music	Composer
Giraffes Can't Dance by Giles Andreae	"Summon the Heroes"	John Williams
Jazzy in the Jungle by Lucy Cousins	Piano Concerto no. 1	Tchaikovsky
Please, Baby, Please by Spike Lee and Tonya Lewis-Lee	"Birks Works"	Dizzy Gillespie
The Kiss That Missed by David Melling	"Gandalf"	Johan de Meij

Keep a running list of music and song combinations as you find selections of your own. You will not only have a growing collection of books to read to children, but also a growing collection of music to accompany the books. Introducing children to music of depth and quality, regardless of the genre, is a gift that engages both sides of the developing brain while connecting with children's emotional intelligence.

Practice

Symphony of Emotion

The word *symphony* usually refers to a multimovement work performed by an orchestra. Symphonies, such as Beethoven's Ninth Symphony, have many pieces and multiple layers. The performance of a symphony brings together these pieces and layers.

Key

Primary learning style: kinesthetic
Domain: language development
Specific academic area: literacy
Educational bonus: social-emotional development (teamwork and sharing) and gross- and fine-motor skill development
Suggested music: none
Materials needed: lots of energy and a willingness to improvise

Much like a symphony, this game is about putting together pieces and layers of information. In the game, adults and groups of children define descriptive words with body movements and sound effects. Each group performs a "symphony of emotion" with these movements and sounds effects.

This game invites all learners—auditory, visual, and kinesthetic—to engage, but it is especially effective for kinesthetic learners, helping them improve their vocabulary and comprehension skills. Critical-thinking skills, problem-solving skills, and creativity also are addressed when playing this game.

The following step-by-step description involves eighteen children and three adults.

1. Separate children and adults into three groups. Each group should consist of six children and one adult.

2. Have each group choose a color. Ask them to keep the color a secret from the other groups.

3. After the groups have chosen their colors, challenge them to pick several emotion words to describe their color. Make sure the adults ask the children questions to help them come up with the words.

4. After each group has chosen several words, ask them to come up with body movements and sounds that represent their words.

5. Have each group perform their movements and sounds while everyone else tries to guess their words.

Variation

As an optional ending, have one adult conduct the symphony by creating a mixture of body movements and sound effects.

I would like to thank Candace Mazur for introducing me to the idea of Symphony of Emotion.

Practice

Symphony of Seasons

Similar to Symphony of
Emotion, Symphony of Sea-
sons is a kinesthetic game
that invites auditory and
visual learners as well. This
game will help you develop
children's literacy skills,
specifically comprehension, along with critical-thinking and problem-
solving skills.

Key

Primary learning style: kinesthetic
Domain: cognitive development
Specific academic area: science (identifying sea-
sons and the natural phenomena of each season)
Educational bonus: literacy (vocabulary expansion
and comprehension) and creativity
Suggested music: none
Materials needed: imagination

1. Separate a large group of children into two or three small
   groups, each with an adult guide.

2. Give each group a season to represent: winter, spring,
   summer, or fall. Ask each group to keep their season a secret
   from the other groups.

3. Using questions and improvisation, have each group become
   a scene from their season. For example, if the group's season
   is winter, ask them to create a winter scene, which might
   include actions like going ice-skating, sitting by a fire, drinking hot chocolate, or decorating a home for a holiday.

4. Make sure each child has a role in the scene.

5. Have each group perform their scene while the other
   groups guess the season and the actions of the scene.

6. To finish the game, have each group share what they enjoyed
   most about each group's performance. This allows children
   to practice retelling a story.

Variations

- Mix the scenes into one performance.

- For more advanced play with older children, choose a season and a location somewhere in the world (winter in Chicago, winter in Tucson, summer in London, or summer in Columbia).

- Build on the game each time you play. Start with a simple scene, and then add details, props, artwork, music, and so on each time you play.

Practice

Symphony of Science

In this symphony game, children and adult guides become the environment. Use what children know about the environment as a place to start and then take the activity further. For example, children who live in a rural setting may have a better grasp of how different elements of nature interact than children in an urban setting. City dwellers may be most familiar with industrial or human-made elements. Here are basic instructions to get you started:

Key

Primary learning style: kinesthetic
Domain: cognitive development
Specific academic area: science (identifying animals, plants, weather, and ecosystems)
Educational bonus: math (counting groups of animals and plants) and cooperation
Suggested music: *Behind the Gardens* by Andreas Vollenweider
Materials needed: music source and room to move

1. Separate a large group into at least three smaller groups of children, each with an adult guide.

2. Create the landscape within the classroom. You could, for example, designate one or two areas as islands and other areas as bays, rivers, or oceans. Use your imagination and include other interesting geographic features, such as volcanoes.

3. Ask each group of children to become a characteristic of the landscape or environment, such as the weather, an animal group, or the plant life. You can also have some groups become the water or currents.

4. Play music that is relaxing but also engaging and emotionally diverse.

5. Guide the children by demonstrating, asking questions, and improvising.

6. When the children become the environment, ask questions about how the different parts of the environment interact, such as "What happens to the seeds of a plant when the wind blows?" or "What happens if rain doesn't stop for a long time?"

7. After all the groups tell their stories through movement and role playing, turn down the music and ask the children what they liked most about the game. Reflect with the children about the experience.

Variations

This process-based game is designed to let you improvise as needed. Consider using this game as a template to explore a book in a new way or to highlight something that is already a part of your classroom curriculum.

Practice

Student-Created Musicals

Student-created musicals
take time, dedication,
and a willingness to truly
engage students. I recom-
mend trying all of the other
games listed in this book
many times before trying
a student-created musical.
That said, I do hope you
will try this; the journey is
beautiful and helps children develop many skills, including communica-
tion skills, compassion, leadership skills, and academic prowess (especially in reading and comprehension). I have worked on student-created
musicals with children from ages three to eighteen. While you must
adapt certain elements so the activity is age appropriate, you will follow
the same basic process for any group of children. Here is a basic outline
of how to create musicals with children.

Key

Primary learning styles: all three learning styles
 are engaged
Domains: all domains are engaged
Specific academic area: any a teacher chooses to
 focus on
Educational bonus: cooperation, teamwork,
 vocabulary development, self-regulation, muscle
 development, self-confidence, creativity, and
 critical thinking
Suggested music: a wide variety of classical,
 popular, and world music
Materials needed: props, if applicable

Step 1: Story Line and Character Creation

You can use an existing story or you can develop an original story.
For the first-time musical director, the first option is probably a better
choice. If you use an existing story, modify it with students' input. If
you choose to use an original story, rely on students to brainstorm all
the elements. Both options will aid children's learning if you are willing
to let children take the lead.

Children often want to use a story they already know. This can be
effective and appropriate if you are willing to adapt the story based
on children's input. I have been very successful using fairytales such

as *Jack and the Beanstalk, Goldilocks and the Three Bears,* and *Snow White and the Seven Dwarfs.* Choose a story that has a positive message and that is socially and emotionally appropriate for the children in your group.

Create characters and explore those characters kinesthetically. For example, ask children to become the characters by acting out scenes within the story line. As you brainstorm with the children, make sure to have a visual aid, such as an interactive whiteboard or chalkboard, for noting ideas and plans. As you talk about and create characters, write down ideas so that children can connect what is being said with what is being written. This is an excellent way to help children begin to read and want to read.

Step 2: Script Creation

Create the story line in small groups if the process would be unwieldy with the entire group. Create the script in auditory, visual, and kinesthetic ways. For example, have children become the words and emotions in the story with their bodies to enhance comprehension. Coming up with body movements related to dance numbers is great as well.

Step 3: Music Creation

This step can vary greatly. First, decide as a group what songs are needed. Usually the main characters each have a song. If the children are very young, most of the songs should be group numbers, as opposed to solos. Brainstorm with the children—using lots of questions—to come up with the words for the songs. Part of this process can be teacher directed, but most of it should be child driven. Children can come up with both interesting words and good melodies. From there, you can take children's melodies and add chords and other essentials to create a basic arrangement. If you do not have a background in music, consider finding someone who does to help.

As another option, use a melody from a song that children already know. This works best with young children. For example, if you were creating a musical of *Jack and the Beanstalk*, you could use the melody of "Twinkle, Twinkle, Little Star" but add children's original lyrics. The song might look something like this:

Jack jumps up the tall beanstalk.
Climbing higher, up he goes.
Through the clouds and higher still.
Wondering where the beanstalk goes.
Jack jumps up the tall beanstalk.
Where he ends up, we don't know.

Involving the children in the creative process is what's most important. Ask children what kind of emotion the music should portray in each scene.

Step 4: Dance and Movement Numbers
Every musical involves some dance. For young children, dances can include gross-motor movements and can be as simple as a set of hand movements. You don't need or want to create a Broadway-level dance routine. Have children come up with some of the movement ideas and incorporate them into parts of the songs, chants, or rhymes. You will notice that children will now remember the general story line, spoken lines, music, and dance routines. What a rich environment and fantastic way to engage the whole brain of a child!

Step 5: Rehearsing
Make sure rehearsals are developmentally appropriate in length; don't forget the attention spans of the children. Use vocabulary that is appropriate for young children, but don't be afraid to introduce new words to expand children's knowledge. Use auditory, visual, and kinesthetic ways to guide the children. Keep rehearsals natural and organic. Remind yourself that it's a process, not an event.

Start with individual scenes. Be sure to think about how to transition from one scene to another. Refer back to the Master Teaching

Principles in part 1 (especially chapter 3, Ask Questions to Develop Critical-Thinking Skills, on page 31, and chapter 4, Improvise to Encourage Creativity, on page 37) to help you guide the children during rehearsal. Questions will help children to really become and understand the characters. Remember that you can make changes to the musical as you go.

Step 6: The Process and the Result

This kind of project normally takes at least two months and as long as four months to complete, depending on how often you rehearse. The process—children's learning and experience—is more important than the result. It's not really important for the production to be a full-scale, professional-quality show. For inspiration and encouragement, visit a student-created musical somewhere in your community. If there are no student-created musicals in your area, search online for "youth musicals" to see a range of examples.

Measurable and Immeasurable Results

THE PLAY-BASED ACTIVITIES, GAMES, and techniques offered in this book will successfully engage children. In today's society, however, success is often measured by specific academic outcomes. Measurable results can be helpful and should be used to confirm that the arts are critical to young children's advanced learning and growth. The research presented in chapter 12 shows that the Life Learning Techniques accelerate pre-K learning and knowledge retention in the core subject areas of literacy, math, and science. They also improve social-emotional development.

Alongside the data in chapter 12, you will find quotations from teachers and parents who have used the Life Learning Techniques and Master Teaching Principles in their homes and classrooms. These quotations give a voice to the data. I encourage you to share the research, outcomes, and quotations from chapter 12 with your local leaders in education, business, and politics. They will likely be most interested in the following two conclusions:

1. Artistic and play-based approaches to learning lead to critical thinking, creativity, and leadership skills.

2. Learning that integrates the arts (including music, dance, visual arts, and drama) improves both academic learning and the development of a positive self-concept.

I hope these findings inspire policy makers to become advocates for early childhood education and arts education. Together we can inspire a paradigm shift that commits all of us to making the next generation creative, compassionate, and communicative. I hope you take this message with you after you finish this book.

Remember, measured results are not the sole reason we should incorporate the methods in this book into our teaching and into children's learning. The most critical things children gain from master teachers—and master teachers from children—cannot be measured. I don't wake up in the morning and think to myself, "How many more statistics I can validate today?" That is not where my passion lies. I focus on doing and being—that is, using the techniques in this book to do my best and be more like a child so I can connect with and guide young children in ways that are organic, trusting, and empowering. I encourage you to do the same. Use the techniques in this book on a daily basis and make them a part of your daily routine. Lastly, I hope you accept my invitation in chapter 13 to live in the eye of the hurricane, for yourself and the children you serve.

Chapter 12

Measured
Student Gains

Research Methodology

My colleagues and I at the Fostering Arts-Mind Education Foundation
conducted and compiled the research that follows. Since its formation
in 2001, the Fostering Arts-Mind Education Foundation has successfully served more than thirty thousand children and families in multiple
settings, including Head Start programs, public preschools, private
preschools, public elementary schools, and charter high schools. Programs from Alabama, Arizona, California, Nevada, New Mexico, New
York, Ohio, Oregon, Puerto Rico, and the District of Columbia have
partnered with the foundation.

The Fostering Arts-Mind Education Foundation conducted the following research from 2001 through 2004. Assessments were conducted
during the 2001–2 and 2003–4 school years, the outcomes of which
were then statistically validated. In the interim 2002–3 school year, the
foundation reorganized its approach to the research, reflected on the
best questions to ask, and revised research methods to improve the clarity of our findings.

The field of three-, four-, and five-year-olds in each school year were divided into two groups. The experimental group, referred to as the Life Learning Technique group (LLT group), included only students exposed to the Life Learning Techniques over the school year. All of the children in the LLT group were in child care programs based in Ohio with access to the Fostering Arts-Mind Education Foundation's services. The teachers of children in the LLT group had two years of ongoing professional development in Life Learning Techniques. The control group consisted of a national cross section of children who were not exposed to the techniques.

Assessments to measure children's capabilities in specific domains took place throughout the 2001–2 and 2003–4 school years. Both the control and experimental groups were assessed with Galileo, a tool created by Dr. Jack Bergan, chief executive officer of Assessment Technology Inc., in Tucson, Arizona (www.ati-online.com). At the time of this research, the assessment tool was the only one of its kind to have been mandated by a state department of education (Ohio Department of Education), and it was the largest database of statistically validated data on young children's growth. The Galileo assessment tool is an ongoing, observation-based software that contains developmentally sequenced lists for capabilities in literacy, math, science, and social-emotional development. The lists in each area vary between fifty-three and seventy-three individual capabilities.

Researchers assessed the progress of children in both the experimental and control groups from beginning levels to more advanced levels in the areas of math, literacy, science, and social-emotional development. The terms *beginning learning category*, *intermediate learning category*, and *advanced learning category* refer to the number of individual learning capabilities a child has mastered at the time of assessment. *Mastery* means a child has demonstrated command of a learning capability various times, not just once. If a child has mastered more than two-thirds of the capabilities in an area, such as literacy, then that child is in the advanced learning category in that area. If a child has mastered one-third or fewer of the capabilities, the child is in the beginning learning category. While we mostly looked at positives—children who progressed from the beginning learning category to the intermediate or advanced learning category—we also looked at how many children in each group were still in the beginning learning category at the end of the school year.

2001–2 Results

The LLT group consisted of 430 children (three-, four-, and five-year-olds) from Athens, Ohio, and Coshocton, Ohio. The control group consisted of a national cross section of 3,355 children tested for literacy, 3,352 children tested for math, and 2,852 children tested for social-emotional development.

Tables 1 through 3 show the number and percentage of three-, four-, and five-year-olds found to be in the advanced learning category as of November 30, 2001, and then as of May 15, 2002. The *increase* shows the growth in the percentage of children reaching the advanced learning category.

At the time of this study, seventy-three individual capabilities were measured for literacy, sixty-four individual capabilities were measured for math, and seventy-one individual capabilities were measured for social-emotional development.

Table 1. Number and percentage of students in the advanced learning category in math

	30 Nov. 2001	15 May 2002	Increase
Control group	235 (7%)	670 (20%)	435 more children ended the school year in the advanced learning category, a 13% increase.
LLT group	17 (4%)	181 (42%)	164 more children ended the school year in the advanced learning category, a 38% increase.

"Breathing has become a daily part of our classroom routine. Our children always hear the classical music and know we are going to do our breathing. It has helped all of us relax and start our day with calm hearts and happy faces! It has been a joy learning these calming techniques. These are lifelong skills I will treasure."

—Head Start teacher, Kno-Ho-Co-Ashland, Coshocton, Ohio

"I enjoy the breathing. The different kinds of breathing help us control stress and calm the little ones when they are overly excited."

—Armida Barajas, Head Start teacher, Child-Parent Centers, Tucson, Arizona

Table 2. Number and percentage of students in the advanced learning category in social-emotional development

	30 Nov. 2001	15 May 2002	Increase
Control group	684 (24%)	1,226 (43%)	542 more children ended the school year in the advanced learning category, a 19% increase.
LLT group	17 (4%)	194 (45%)	177 more children ended the school year in the advanced learning category, a 41% increase.

"I love the improvising because we can follow the children's lead, and [each activity] then becomes their activity, their game. This leads to all kinds of areas that are important to a child's learning and development."

—Head Start teacher, Child-Parent Centers, Tucson, Arizona

Table 3. Number and percentage of students in the advanced learning category in literacy

	30 Nov. 2001	15 May 2002	Increase
Control group	403 (12%)	1,074 (32%)	671 more children ended the school year in the advanced learning category, a 20% increase.
LLT group	21 (5%)	129 (30%)	108 more children ended the school year in the advanced learning category, a 25% increase.

"I just wanted to let you know how well the Life Learning Techniques are working with my four-year-old son, Jack. The other day his two-year-old sister, Abby, asked him to read her a story. 'Okay,' Jack said, 'you sit beside me . . . now breathe in, breathe out.' Then looking down at the book, he made up a name for the book and said, 'This is the title page, and the author is. . . . Well, I don't know why somebody wrote it.' One other time, Abby was trying to put together a train track and was getting very upset because it wouldn't work. Jack said, 'Abby, do this . . . breathe in . . . breathe out, and then you can do it.'"

—Head Start parent, Athens, Ohio

2003–4 Results

During the 2003–4 school year, science was added in our research, and the size of the LLT group and the control group increased. The LLT group consisted of 600 three-, four-, and five-year-olds from Athens, Ohio, and Akron, Ohio. The control group consisted of a national cross section of three-, four-, and five-year-olds and included 6,150 children tested for science, 6,150 children tested for math, 6,941 tested children for social-emotional development, and 6,972 children tested for literacy.

Tables 4 and 5 in sample A show the percentage of children who were in the advanced learning category as of November 30, 2003, and then as of June 1, 2004. The increase shows the growth in the percentage of children reaching that level. Tables 6 and 7 in sample B show the percentage of children who were in the intermediate or advanced learning category as of November 30, 2003, and then as of June 1, 2004. The increase shows the growth in the percentage of children reaching that level. Table 8 in sample C shows the percentile rank of children at the end of the school year (May 30, 2004).

At the time of this study, fifty-seven individual capabilities were measured for science, fifty-three individual capabilities were measured for math, sixty-two individual capabilities were measured for social-emotional development, and seventy-one individual capabilities were measured for literacy.

SAMPLE A

Table 4. Number and percentage of students in the advanced learning category in science

	30 Nov. 2003	1 Jun. 2004	Increase
Control group	123 (2%)	1,476 (24%)	1,353 more children ended the school year in the advanced learning category, a 22% increase.
LLT group	78 (13%)	300 (50%)	222 more children ended the school year in the advanced learning category, a 37% increase.

Table 5. Number and percentage of students in the advanced learning category in math

	30 Nov. 2003	1 Jun. 2004	Increase
Control group	431 (7%)	2,645 (43%)	2,214 more children ended the school year in the advanced learning category, a 36% increase.
LLT group	30 (5%)	282 (47%)	252 more children ended the school year in the advanced learning category, a 42% increase.

"I have utilized the relaxation and breathing techniques for myself and shared them with staff and colleagues. They help me manage the stress in my demanding work."

—Sandra de La Cerda, Head Start curriculum specialist,
Child-Parent Centers, Tucson, Arizona

Sample B

Table 6. Number and percentage of students in the advanced or intermediate learning category in math

	30 Nov. 2003	1 Jun. 2004	Increase
Control group	123 (38%)	1,476 (84%)	1,353 more children ended the school year in the advanced or intermediate learning category, a 46% increase.
LLT group	210 (35%)	528 (88%)	318 more children ended the school year in the advanced or intermediate learning category, a 53% increase.

"As a teacher, I work with children who come from a variety of backgrounds. I love giving the children confidence in themselves, letting them know that they are champions and very special individuals. One mother said her son Brandon came home saying, 'Mommy, did you know I have a brain?' I have several children that I had to remind throughout the day to breathe and relax to calm them down. I see these same children doing it by themselves now."

—Head Start teacher, Tri-County Head Start, Athens, Ohio

Table 7. Number and percentage of students in the advanced or intermediate learning category in literacy

	30 Nov. 2003	1 Jun. 2004	Increase
Control group	3,137 (45%)	5,856 (84%)	2,719 more children ended the school year in the advanced or intermediate learning category, a 39% increase.
LLT group	180 (30%)	492 (82%)	312 more children ended the school year in the advanced or intermediate learning category, a 52% increase.

"Taking educational risks is what I enjoyed the most in my sessions with the foundation. I love the workshops, which were like retreats. The techniques presented are things I can use in my personal life as well as professional."

—Ana Rocio Navarro, Head Start teacher,
Child-Parent Centers, Tucson, Arizona

SAMPLE C

The LLT group performed at a higher level than the control group when comparing end-of-the-year percentile rank. Note that this is a percentile, not a percentage. A percentile is a comparative measure used in statistics and other fields where data is evaluated. Percentiles are commonly applied to test scores. Percentiles show rank. So if an individual were to rank in the 65th percentile, it would mean that 65 percent of the people being ranked fall below and 35 percent rank higher. The higher the percentile the higher the rank.

Table 8. Percentile rank of students at the end of the school year by subject area

	Math	Social-emotional development	Literacy	Science
	30 May 2004	30 May 2004	30 May 2004	30 Jun. 2004
Control group	85.03	68.74	78.04	70.99
LLT group	93.45	82.27	92.90	87.0
Difference	+ 8.42	+ 13.53	+ 14.86	+ 16.01

"The whole kissing the brain . . . the children love it. And every time they do something great, I'm telling them they're so smart and that they are champions. The kids love it! They smile so big. Everyone is trying to do something great so they can hear me say, 'Kiss your brain.' While you are affirming young children in a silly and appropriate way, you can also engage in early literacy skills, and perhaps best of all, you will be doing so in a kinesthetic manner! Remember, many children learn by doing it or becoming it! My only note of caution is that once you begin kissing your brain, the kissing will, in most cases, become part of your daily routine. In fact, I have heard many children tell their parents 'you need to kiss your brain,' which is usually an accurate assessment for the parent in question!"

—Heat Start teacher, Tri-County Head Start, Athens, Ohio

Significance

The data clearly indicates that children with teachers who have been exposed to the Life Learning Techniques show more progress than children with teachers who do not. Impressively, the LLT group began with a smaller percentage of children in the advanced learning category than the control groups but ended up with a higher percentage in the advanced learning category in math and social-emotional development and, statistically, in literacy by the end of the school year. In the 2001–2 school year, for example, 94 percent of children in the LLT group but only 66 percent of children in the control group ended the school year in the intermediate or advanced learning category in math. For literacy, 76 percent of children in the LLT group but only 70 percent of children in the control group ended the school year in the intermediate or advanced learning category.

Children in the LLT group who started with a smaller base of academic knowledge ended up ahead of or even with children who started out with a larger base of academic knowledge. Plus, a smaller percentage of children in the LLT group remained in the beginning learning category than children in the control groups. In the 2003–4 school year, for example, 30 percent of children in the control group but only 13 percent of children in the LLT group ended the school year in the beginning learning category in science. For social-emotional development, 14 percent of children in the control group but only 8 percent of children in the LLT group ended the school year in the beginning learning category.

The data may excite you, and it should. The numbers are impressive and will hopefully lead more programs to use the Life Learning Techniques or similar techniques with children.

Chapter 13

· · · · · · · · · · ·

An Invitation to Live in the Eye of the Storm

The eye of a hurricane, approximately twenty to forty miles across, is in direct contrast to the raging storm that encircles it. Although winds are dangerously high in the dense wall of thunderstorms surrounding the eye, the eye itself—the axis—is relatively calm with light winds. The eye also has a low surface pressure and warm temperature compared to the surrounding storm, and it enjoys little or no precipitation. In many hurricane eyes, the sky is clearly visible by day and the stars are clearly visible by night.

We can choose to be the eye of any situation. We can remain calm yet focused and see everything around us with clarity. We might sometimes enter into the storm of emotional imbalance, dishonesty, lies, and negativity—sometimes by choice and other times by no fault of our own—but the eye is always there as a place of solitude, peace, and power. I am not saying it is easy to live in the eye of the storm. It is, however, simple.

The most curious things happen when we least expect them. About two-thirds of the way into crafting this book, my life was on autopilot, in a good way. Smooth sailing was ahead, and joy was everywhere. I occasionally entered storms of frustration and sadness, but these were small in comparison to the joy I surround myself with. Then, all of a sudden, I was consumed by a hurricane the likes of which I had not experienced before—my wife, the love of my life, experienced a heart attack. An energetic, happy, and vibrant young woman wasn't supposed to have that happen to her. Because of this stress, many things that normally brought me joy brought me nothing at all.

In truth, I stopped letting the joy in. Joy was there for the taking, but I was no longer in the eye of the storm. I lived in the storm all the time, which means most of my energy was spent merely surviving. When all you do is survive, you regress to baser instincts.

Today I am back to living in the eye. To mimic Yoda, "Rocket science . . . hrrmm . . . it is not." Marie is healthy and completely recovered, and we are healthier than ever because we used the experience as an opportunity to expand our potential. Once I was able to see clearly again, I realized that entering the eye is simple—as simple as deciding to be grateful, thankful, and excited about life—but it is not always easy. It is not always easy to see things positively, but it is simple. It is simple to learn and to teach, but it is not easy. These things can, however, become easier.

Children tend to live in the eye unless they are mistreated or abused. For many, living in the eye is a natural state of being, a normal mode of life experience. As adults we must embrace the importance of living like a child. We must relearn how to live in the eye of our own experiences so that we are capable, inspiring, and inviting for young children. The key to living in the eye involves relaxation and focus.

There are hundreds of relaxation techniques, and I've shared some basic techniques that you can begin to use immediately. Two fundamental elements for any group of relaxation techniques are positive affirmation and breathing. No matter what techniques you use, these two elements must be included to create a positive, evolving, complete, and smoothly functioning individual. Some people describe this mind-body state as being "in the zone." Call it what you want; breathing deeply and smoothly coupled with a routine of strong affirmation keeps the body relaxed and the mind alert.

Living in the eye of life is all about living in the moment. Of course, planning for the future is also a good idea, but being in the moment is where we thrive. We can and should learn from the past, but appreciating what is happening right now is a key to success and is how happy children live.

Yes, I said the *S* word, *success*. What does that word mean? How do you define success as an early childhood educator? As a musician? As a lawyer, doctor, or financial consultant? You decide. My own definition has something to do with the question "How do I empower others?" Notice that I didn't use the words *save* or *help*; I used the word *empower*. People like to be empowered. It feels good to get up, get things done, and achieve. Achievements do not have to shake the world. They only have to shake *your* world. From there you can begin to evolve and can begin to empower others by example. Lead by example, and use the Master Teaching Principles and Life Learning Techniques as tools to help you to recognize what others need.

Being in the moment and doing things to empower others is much like being relaxed and focused at the same time. It is a lot like living in the eye of the storm—always moving, but with a calm that allows clarity. The *art of being* has its foundation in affirmation, and the *science of doing* has its foundation in visualization. Imagination or visualization connects the *art of being* with the *science of doing*.

Ask yourself, "Who am I?" and "Is this who I want to be?" Then ask children who they want to be. Curiosity is one of the most wonderful human characteristics. Remind yourself to continue to embrace your own curiosity for life and to allow children to explore within the eye.

I hope you find the peace and power of the eye in your life, with your family, and with the children you serve.

Appendix

✿ ✿ ✿ ✿ ✿ ✿ ✿

Sample Music Lists

SLOW CLASSICAL AND BAROQUE MUSIC selections are appropriate for times when you want to calm children or improve focus. Fast classical and baroque selections are appropriate for times when you want to engage children at high energy levels. Music selections marked as high frequency will give the mind and body the most rapid recharge; these selections cross the right and left sides of the brain and provide balance and energy to the brain and body at the same time (Ostrander and Schroeder 1994). Treat this list of music as a starting point. Add your own favorites over time to create a music list that is your own.

Slow Classical and Baroque Selections (approximately sixty beats per minute)

COMPILATIONS

Compilation Title	Description
Adagio collections	Search for "Adagio collections" on the Internet to find many compilations of slow-tempo music
The Mozart Effect, Volume 2	Ideal for rest and relaxation
The Mozart Effect, Volume 5	Ideal for deep rest and rejuvenation
Mozart for Mothers-to-Be	A set of lullabies
One for the Children	Includes slow selections and music in both Spanish and English (available from the Southern Arizona AEYC organization at www.sazaeyc.org)
Superlearning Music	A mix of selections at sixty beats per minute
*The Tree and the Wind**	Contains back-to-back slow selections for easy classroom and home use

NONCOMPILATIONS

Composer	Title of Selection
Bach	Air on the G String
Bach	Largo from Harpsichord Concerto in C Major
Bach	Largo from Harpsichord Concerto in F Minor
Caudioso	Largo from Concerto for Mandolin and Strings
Corelli	Largo from Concerto no. 10 in F, op. 5

Giazotto	Adagio in G Minor for Strings
Mozart	Third movement from Eine Kleine Nachtmusik
Pachelbel	Canon in D
Telemann	Largo from Double Fantasia in G Major for Harpsichord
Vivaldi	Largo from Concerto in C Major for Mandolin, Strings, and Harpsichord
Vivaldi	Largo from Concerto in D Major Guitar and Strings
Vivaldi	Largo from "Winter" from *The Four Seasons*

CONTEMPORARY COMPOSERS

Duncan, William	*Exultate* (guitar)
Gagnon, Andre	"Lullaby for My Mother" from *The St. Lawrence*
Hoffman, Janalea	*Deep Daydreams* (electronic instrumental music)
Hoffman, Janalea	*Mind-Body Tempo* (piano and orchestra)

Fast Classical and Baroque Selections (120 beats per minute)

The actual tempo varies slightly, as it should with live music.

COMPILATION

Compilation Title	Description
The Tree and the Wind*	Contains back-to-back fast selections for easy classroom and home use

Noncompilations

Composer	Title of Selection
Beethoven	Concerto for Violin and Orchestra in D Major, op. 61
Brahms	Concerto for Violin and Orchestra in D Major, op. 77
Chopin	Waltzes
Haydn	Symphony no. 67 in F Major
Haydn	Symphony no. 68 in B-flat Major
Mozart	Concerto for Piano and Orchestra no. 18 in B-flat Major
Mozart	Concerto for Piano and Orchestra no. 23 in A Major
Mozart	Concerto for Violin and Orchestra no. 1 in B-flat Major (high frequency)
Mozart	Concerto for Violin and Orchestra no. 2 in D Major (high frequency)
Mozart	Concerto for Violin and Orchestra no. 3 in G Major (high frequency)
Mozart	Concerto for Violin and Orchestra no. 4 in D Major (high frequency)
Mozart	Concerto for Violin and Orchestra no. 5 in A Major
Mozart	Divertimento for String Quartet in B-flat Major
Mozart	Divertimento for String Quartet in D Major
Mozart	Divertimento for String Quartet in F Major
Mozart	Sinfonia Concertante in E-flat Major for Violin, Viola, and Orchestra (high frequency)
Mozart	String Quartets nos. 1–14 in various keys (high frequency)
Mozart	String quartet arrangements in various keys (high frequency)

Mozart	String quartet fugues and rondos in various keys (high frequency)
Mozart	Symphony no. 29 in A Major (high frequency)
Mozart	Symphony no. 32 in G Major (high frequency)
Mozart	*Haffner* Symphony no. 35 in D Major
Mozart	*Prague* Symphony no. 38 in D Major
Mozart	Symphony no. 39 in E-flat Major (high frequency)
Mozart	Symphony no. 40 in G Minor (high frequency)
Tchaikovsky	Concerto no. 1 for Piano and Orchestra in B-flat Minor, op. 23
Tchaikovsky	Concerto for Violin in D Major, op. 35

Music for Moving

When looking for music to move to, you have many options. What follows is a very short list of selections I often use, some of which I produced. Start listening to music from different cultures and countries, such as gypsy music, and create your own movement music library.

COMPILATIONS

Composer/Producer	Title
Clement, Debbie	*Debbie's Ditties . . . for Little Kiddies*
Clement, Debbie	*Debbie's Ditties 2: Much Fun*
Clement, Debbie	*Debbie's Ditties 3: At the Library*
Clement, Debbie	*Debbie's Ditties 4: Come Dance S'more*
Clement, Debbie	*Debbie's Ditties 5: Jump, Jam, Jive*

Clement, Debbie   *Debbie's Ditties 6: The Handwriting Mix*

Feldman, Enrique C.   *Vida Rica**

Feldman, Enrique C.   *Moving to Learn**

GENERIC STYLES

Big band	Jewish
Blues	Merengue
Funk	Middle Eastern
Gypsy	Salsa
Jazz	Tango

*Produced by the Fostering Arts-Mind Education Foundation, www.famefoundation.org.

References

American Heart Association. 2010. "NFL Play 60 Challenge." Updated July 6. www.heart.org/HEARTORG/Educator/FortheClassroom /NFLPlay60Challenge/NFL-PLAY-60-Challenge-Page_UCM_304278_ Article.jsp.

Anderson, Scheree, Jeanette Henke, Maureen McLaughlin, Mary Ripp, and Patricia Tuffs. 2000. "Using Background Music to Enhance Memory and Improve Learning." Master's thesis, Saint Xavier University. www.eric .ed.gov/ERICWebPortal/custom/portlets/recordDetails/detailmini.jsp?_ nfpb=true&_&ERICExtSearch_SearchValue_0=ED437663&ERICExtSear ch_SearchType_0=no&accno=ED437663.

Campbell, Don. 2001. *The Mozart Effect: Tapping the Power of Music to Heal the Body, Strengthen the Mind, and Unlock the Creative Spirit.* New York: HarperCollins.

Carlson, Judith, Janalea Hoffman, Dorothy Gray, and Alex Thompson. 2004. "A Musical Interlude: Using Music and Relaxation to Improve Reading Performance." *Intervention in School and Clinic* 39 (4): 246–50.

Chapman, Gary. 1992. *The Five Love Languages: How to Express Heartfelt Commitment to Your Mate.* Chicago: Northfield Publishing.

Cosgrove-Mather, Bootie. 2002. "It's a Fat, Fat, Fat World." CBS News, May 15. http://www.cbsnews.com/stories/2002/05/15/health/main509230 .shtml.

Davies, Michaela, Richard D. Roberts, and Lazar Slankov. 1998. "Emotional Intelligence: In Search of an Elusive Construct." *Journal of Personality and Social Psychology* 75 (4): 989–1015.

Gedgaudas, Nora. 2009. *Primal Body—Primal Mind.* Portland, OR: Primal Body Primal Mind Publishing.

Kemple, Kristin M., and Stacy M. Ellis. 2009. "Peer-Related Social Competence in Early Childhood: Supporting Interaction and Relationships." In *Informing Our Practice: Useful Research on Young Children's Development*, eds. Eva L. Essa and Melissa M. Burnham, 5–12. Washington, DC: National Association for the Education of Young Children.

Kosslyn, Steven. 1995. "The Brain's Mind's Eye." *On the Brain* 4 (1): 1–3. http://www.csulb.edu/~cwallis/482/kosslyn.html.

Kraus, Stephen. 2006. "Success Lessons from the Winter Olympics: Visualization." Posted February 19. http://www.selfgrowth.com/articles/Kraus7.html.

Lobstein, Tim, Neville Rigby, and Rachel Leach. 2005. "International Obesity Task Force EU Platform on Diet, Physical Activity, and Health." Briefing paper, Brussels, Belgium. www.iotf.org/media/euobesity3.pdf.

McCraty, Rollin, Bob Barrios-Choplin, Mike Atkinson, and Dana Tomasino. 1998. "The Effects of Different Types of Music on Mood, Tension, and Mental Clarity." *Alternative Therapies* 4 (1): 75–84.

National Association for Sport and Physical Education. 2002. *Active Start*. Reston, VA: National Association for Sport and Physical Education.

Ostrander, Sheila, and Lynn Schroeder. 1979. *Superlearning*. New York: Delacorte.

———. 1994. *Superlearning 2000*. New York: Delacorte.

Parish, Loraine, and Mary Rudisill. 2006. "HAPPE: Toddlers in Physical Play." *Beyond the Journal*, May. www.naeyc.org/files/yc/file/200605/ParishBTJ.pdf.

Salimpoor, Valorie N., Mitcher Benovoy, Kevin Larcher, Alain Dagher, and Robert Zatorre. 2011. "Anatomically Distinct Dopamine Release during Anticipation and Experience of Peak Emotion to Music." *Nature Neuroscience* 14 (2): 257–62.

About the Author

✻ ✻ ✻ ✻ ✻ ✻ ✻

ENRIQUE C. FELDMAN IS THE FOUNDER and director of education for the nonprofit Fostering Arts-Mind Education Foundation (www.famefoundation.org). As the foundation's guide, Enrique directs and delivers services to thousands of children and families each year and empowers teachers and parents with Life Learning Techniques. He is also the director of Evolved Learning Conferences (www.evolvedlearning.com). Enrique was a professor of music and education at the University of Arizona from 1992 through 1997 and served on faculty at the University of Wisconsin–Madison from 1990 through 1992. He has also been a guest faculty member at the Wisconsin Summer Music Clinic, the Brevard Center for Music, and the Interlochen Center for the Arts. He holds a bachelor's degree in music from the University of Arizona in Tucson and a master's degree in education and music performance from the University of Illinois at Urbana–Champaign.

A two-time Grammy nominated composer and artist, Enrique, or "Hank" as he's known in the music world, is also a composer, conductor, and performing artist (www.hankfeldman.com). A classically trained musician, he typically performs in the styles of Latin jazz, blues, and world beat. His most recent work as a composer was for the award-winning film *Cruzando* (www.cruzandothemovie.com). As an artist, he has performed in venues across the globe, from the Franz Liszt Hall in Budapest, Hungary, to the outdoor Red Rocks Amphitheatre in Denver, Colorado. He has produced and performed in seven CD recordings and has pursued additional artistic endeavors, including conducting musicals and directing student musicals with preschool through fifth-grade students. In the early childhood world, he presents internationally, nationally, regionally, and locally. He has presented at the National Association for the Education of Young Children national conference for six consecutive years.

Enrique is married to pianist Marie Sierra, and together they enjoy the arts, traveling, and the simple pleasures of life with their children, Samantha, fifteen, and Nicky, eleven.